To:

From:

Date:

THE MINISTRY OF THE
APOSTLE

THE MINISTRY OF THE
APOSTLE

TEACHER

EVANGELIST

APOSTLE

PROPHET

PASTOR

Discover the Truth About the Apostolic Movement
Guillermo Maldonado

Our Vision

*To take the Word of God everywhere it is needed
and to spiritually feed God's people through
preaching, teaching, and books.*

The Ministry of the Apostle
Discover the truth about the apostolic movement

ISBN: 1-59272-236-9

First Edition 2006

Cover Design by:
ERJ Publications

Published by:
ERJ Publications
13651 SW 143 Ct., Suite 101, Miami, FL 33186
Tel: (305) 233-3325 - Fax: (305) 675-5770

Category:
Apostolic

Printed by:
ERJ Publications, USA

Printed in Colombia

Dedication

With deepest and heart-felt appreciation, I want to dedicate this book to an apostle who is very special and close to my heart. He is my teacher and counselor. He has taught me excellence, wisdom, perseverance, and love. His life and love have inspired and encouraged me to face every challenge that has come my way since the beginning of my ministry; to the apostle of apostles, Jesus of Nazareth.

Acknowledgement

I can think of no better time than this to thank my spiritual sons and daughters who believed in me and who gave of their time and talent to make this project a reality. Thank you for your prayers, faithfulness, and service; and because you understood that writing this book was essential to the restoration of the ministry of the apostle within the body of Christ.

Index

Index

Prologue

T he office of pastor, evangelist, teacher, and prophet have been visible, but where the apostle is concerned, there hasn't been much knowledge of what a true apostle is or what his responsibilities are. Having had the pleasure of hosting Guillermo in my home, and through his relationship with my son, Richard, the President of Oral Roberts University, I immediately felt his spirit and compassion for God's people. However, what hit my spirit is his passion for the Hispanic community—he wants them to have everything God has for them. Guillermo's desire for those who want more in every area of life—spiritually, physically, and financially—led him to his relationship with our ministry and Oral Roberts University. It reminded me of my passion to build God an University—on His authority and filled with His spirit—a place where born-again believers could become doctors, lawyers, ministers, athletes, politicians; thus, filling positions of greatness in their lives—a place that would educate the whole man so Christians could have a voice in the world.

His great desire to see Jesus become real in the lives and families of the Hispanic people is contagious and exhilarating. With his great work in the Miami area and his evangelistic work throughout the world, it is apparent that he not only knows about the office of the apostle but he is an apostle for the Spanish speaking people worldwide. He balances his church and evangelistic work as beautifully as I have ever seen—with his strength and passion for the local church and his fire for the salvation of the lost with the full weight of his gifting for evangelism ever driving him to new and untapped avenues for a lost and dying world. This book on the office and calling of the apostle in the five-fold ministry is a must read for you. When you finish reading this book, you will have a greater understanding of the calling of the apostle and of the five-fold ministry; it will bless you as it has blessed me. I believe something good will happen to you after you take in all of what God has poured into this book through his servant Guillermo Maldonado; a book which will have a special place in my personal library.

Dr. Oral Roberts
Founder and Chancellor
Oral Roberts University

Commentary

A postleship is a much discussed, sometimes confused topic. Often, when we hear a wrong message or a bad report, we toss out the good bits with the bad. Now, Pastor Guillermo Maldonado has written a rock-solid book on apostleship—the most comprehensive I have ever read. It is enlightened and encouraging; it is the missing piece of the puzzle. Pastor Maldonado is an apostle who writes authentically, from revelation and personal experience. If you're looking for a special book on the subject for your library, I can confidently say, "This is it!"

Dr. Marilyn Hickey
Marilyn Hickey Ministries

Introduction

The church has experienced different stages since it was established. The devil, the radical enemy of every Christian, has been hard at work trying to extinguish the light and hide the salt the church has for the world. He creates lies, confusion, laziness, lethargy, and deceit; he steals the identity, purpose, and the gifts of God's children in his efforts to prevent their light from shining. Through all of these, God never disappeared from the scene; He never walked away. He has always provided for His children by giving them what they needed to stand as mighty pillars of truth and salvation.

Half way through the twentieth century, God started to restore the different areas and roles of the Body of Christ. These roles were dormant and down-graded, but today, these are being restored and activated. Between 1940 and 1950, God restored the ministry of the pastor. The years between 1950 and 1960 were years of restoration for the evangelistic ministry. Between 1960 and 1970, the Lord restored the ministry of the teacher. The same thing happened with the prophetic ministry during the 1980s. Since the beginning of 1990, God has been at work restoring the ministry of the Apostle. In every church around the world, we see this gifted servant of God being raised and sent—equipped with a strategic master plan—to strengthen and build the body of Christ.

God has injected us into a time of reformation and restoration of all things. He is taking us from the old wine to the new wine by destroying religious paradigms and stagnancy and by destroying and removing every obstacle that stands in the way of the advancement of His Kingdom. To accomplish this task, God commissioned a very special type of man who is gifted with different characteristics; a man who is bold; a visionary and a pioneer with a fighting spirit. A man with the heart of a father that is full of divine wisdom to build.

An apostle is a man who has a deep intimate relationship with the King; someone who knows God and which path to follow. He is someone who receives the revelations of His Word directly from the throne. This man fears the Lord; he is an aggressive, audacious, intrepid, persevering, and patient man who believes in teamwork. An apostle lives to accomplish the agenda of the Kingdom, not his personal agenda. Everything that was mentioned is given to him by the grace of God to edify the body of Christ, to extend and establish the Kingdom of God, and to cause a spiritual reformation capable of penetrating every layer of society, race, culture, and language around the world. His ultimate goal is to prepare the way for the second coming of the Son of God.

However, while God restores the ministry of the apostle, as it happened with the other ministries, Satan is working hard to destroy it. If he cannot destroy it, he will cause confusion, dishonor, shame, disgrace, doubt, and create lies to try and eliminate or diminish its influence. Also, Christians, with their bad testimonies, often risk the veracity of the work and will of God. There are many genuine apostles today who were raised and sent by God but who are also being attacked by the people they are trying to serve; this is happening because the people do not understand what they are doing. Also, there are men who were commissioned by a committee of their peers and many self-appointed apostles who do not have the fear of the Lord; their hearts and minds are blinded by their hunger for power, recognition, and self-praise.

You might ask, "If God restored the ministry of the apostle, how can I recognize the genuine true apostle? The reason this book was written was to clear up any doubts, to answer your questions, and to set the record straight on the subject of the ministry of the apostle, its characteristics, roles, signs, and purpose. For instance, when an individual begins to work as a bank teller, he will be trained to recognize counterfeit bills. The purpose for this training is to teach him the different signs and symbols that should be present in real paper money and which are extremely difficult to reproduce. Just like U.S. currency, every ministry has a very distinct seal or mark that makes it unique and unequal to the rest. The apostle has a seal that was given by God; many try to duplicate or imitate it, but it will never be the same as the original. Through the pages of this book, you will be trained to recognize the mark, seal, and characteristics which are unique to a genuine apostle of God. You will learn about the apostolic mentality: how the apostle thinks, what his heart is like, what his mission is, what tools he will use to build the church, and much more.

The Lord restored the five ministerial offices of Ephesians 4.11; these are the fist of God used to destroy the works of the devil, and the hand of God which saves, delivers, and edifies the body of Christ. With the full restoration of the five-fold ministries, there is nothing that can stop or prevent the advancement of the Kingdom of God.

"14For the earth will be filled with the knowledge of the glory of the LORD, as the waters cover the sea."
Habakkuk 2.14

1

The Apostolic Reformation and the Flow of the New Wine

G od is bringing a reformation to His church throughout the world. A new generation is being raised and is now crossing over from the old wine to the new wine. Old and obsolete structures are being destroyed in order to make room for the new move of the Holy Spirit. That is why God is restoring the ministry of the apostle in such a way that it will allow this new generation to cause the apostolic reformation and the powerful flow of the new wine. Today, much is said about revivals and how wonderful it is to experience one. However, God is more interested in a reformation because it is by far more radical, deep, permanent, and it reaches the entire church, not just a city or country. For this to be accomplished, it is important for us to carefully study the meaning of a reformation and how the new wine flows.

What is more important to God: revival or reformation?

God wants to bring a revival to His people. However, a revival is not a priority for Him because it is limited to one person, church, city, or nation; its target is never at a global level, and it does not have the global impact that will take the church to another level. A revival is limited to a specific geographical area, and it occurs at a specific time, as it happened in Pensacola, Toronto, and Argentina. The proof lies in the fact that after the revival, there was no legacy left, and leaders were not trained to continue the move of the Holy Spirit in future generations.

On the other hand, a reformation is not limited to a specific area; its objective is to radically impact the body of Christ; every race, city, nation, continent, and culture around the world. The apostolic reformation was designed by God to bring a radical change in the way Christians think and live. This does not mean we do not believe in revivals. We want revivals; we pray for God to bring one, but a reformation has a greater and long-lasting impact. Furthermore, a revival does not include a reformation, but when there is a reformation, a revival is inevitable because it aligns our body, soul, and spirit with the will of God which ultimately allows the Holy Spirit to flow with greater freedom.

What is a reformation?

In Greek, the word **reformation** is *"diorthosis"*; it means: making straight, restoring to its natural and normal condition something that in some way got out of line; it also means an amendment that puts things in order.

An example of a reformation is the Law of Moses which was given by God at Mount Sinai; it symbolized what He was going to do through Jesus. This law had a specific time frame which ended with the birth of Christ and His new covenant with the Father. When Jesus carried out His sacrifice at the cross, He caused a radical and traumatic change in every area of life and through the entire human race. Jesus caused the first apostolic reformation!

"10For [the ceremonies] deal only with clean and unclean meats and drinks and different washings, [mere] external rules and regulations for the body imposed to tide the worshipers over until the time of setting things straight [of reformation, of the complete new order when Christ, the Messiah, shall establish the reality of what these things foreshadow--a better covenant]." Hebrews 9.10—Amplified Bible

God chose this day for His church to enter the new order at a global level; it is a time when those things that are imperfect, inadequate, or twisted can be replaced by something better. The new wine replaces the old wine; it brings a completely new way of doing things to the body of Christ.

Reformation means to make structural adjustments; to rectify and straighten out what had deviated and place it back in its proper form and path. The image we should keep in mind when we hear the word "reformation" can be compared to the work performed by a chiropractor—he treats different illnesses by manipulating the vertebrates in the spinal column. These vertebrae changes affect the function of the body's internal organs and the external appearance of the individual. It is important for the church to also experience strong vertebrae changes which will eventually affect every internal and external area and improve their function as the body of Christ.

There is another Greek word that also describes reformation, and it is *"metamorphoo"*: it means to transfigure, transform, and change. In the Bible, this word appears in the letter of Paul to the Romans:

"2...do not be conformed to this world, but be transformed..." Romans 12.2

A Biblical definition for reformation is: the rectification or amendment that causes a restoration where everything that is incorrect or inadequate is substituted by something better. This new method will cause dramatic and radical changes in people and in the system because it will align us with the good and perfect will of God. The end result will be a revolution where the people will be transformed, transfigured, and changed into better individuals and believers willing to win the world for Christ.

A reformation is not an evolution but a revolution in every way: physical, emotional, and spiritual.

Why is the apostolic reformation so powerful?

- The apostolic reformation is powerful because it brings with it the mighty flow of the new wine; it prepares the new wineskins to receive it so the new wine will not be wasted or lost.

- The apostolic reformation is powerful because it brings forth God's fatherhood and prepares spiritual children with a flexible mentality capable of continuing the work of making sure that the new wine overflows into the present and future generations.

"[37]... no one puts new wine into old wineskins; or else the new wine will burst the wineskins and be spilled, and the wineskins will be ruined." Luke 5.37

What is the new wine?

The new wine is the powerful flow of the power of the Holy Spirit; it flows like a river to save, heal, deliver, and touch our society by revealing the Heavenly Father. It is important to emphasize that the new wine must come first because it is only after its arrival that the old can be removed and replaced.

Why do we need the new wine?

The new wine comes to replace the religious traditions, obsolete methods, and old mentalities or patterns of thinking; to replace negative paradigms, old and incorrect philosophies, negative attitudes, and the old patterns that have been operating in the church.

What must happen for the new wine to come?

The new wine needs new wineskins in order to flow properly. If it is poured into an old wineskin, it will break it and overflow uncontrollably. The wine will be lost like it happened in past revivals where the miracles and manifestations were visible. However, because the generation that witnessed that revival was not prepared to continue the movement—it was not educated through discipleship, and leaders were not trained or equipped to handle it—the revival was lost. A reformation causes the new wine to flow, but it also prepares willing vessels who can guarantee that it will continue to flow and cause the revival to be permanent and world-wide, instead of temporary and at the local level.

Some leaders adopt new methods before changing the wineskin or container, and that is why they are unable to reach their goals. To achieve effective and permanent results, we must change the wineskin, first. In other words, we must change the way we think and begin to apply the new method. The wineskin must be flexible and have the ability to be stretched far enough to contain the new ideas, patterns of thought, and the methods of the new wine.

What are the essential characteristics of a "new wine" man or woman?

1. They have the revelation of the Father.

The revelation of our Heavenly Father is vital to being able to fully enjoy the powerful flow of the new wine. This revelation includes knowing, at a personal level, that He is my Father, that I am His son, and that He loves me.

2. They do not live by traditional legalities.

The "new wine" believer does not join old patterns of thought or man's traditions. He does not establish new moral codes or tries to impose improper traditions on the people. The new wineskin has, as its foundation, the flow of the life of God which delivers and enables him to enjoy life without interruption. Of course, it is understood that his freedom is in Christ, not in living freely and without limits.

3. **They know how to hear and obey God's voice.**

"¹⁴For as many as are led by the Spirit of God, these are sons of God." Romans 8.14

The new wine believer has a close and personal relationship with His Heavenly Father; he knows how to listen and obey His voice. These are essential characteristics needed to contain and effectively transfer the new wine.

4. **They are flexible.**

One characteristic of the new wine believer is that he is always ready to operate by faith and make the necessary changes in mind and heart. He is open to new ideas and patterns of thoughts, and he is willing to move in the direction shown to him by the Holy Spirit— without resisting or questioning His guidance.

5. **They recognize who is in authority—the headship.**

"³But I want you to know that the head of every man is Christ, the head of woman is man, and the head of Christ is God." 1 Corinthians 11.3

Another characteristic of a new wineskin believer is that he understands that the pattern or design of God to operate in the new wine is a governmental structure that is correct. In other words, this structure must include: the headship—a man—shoulders that sustain it, and a body that obeys it. Consequently, a man receives the revelation of the will of God and directs his leaders—the shoulders—to carry out his instructions in the body.

We are living in new wine times! It is time for the old wineskin to leave and lead the way to the new. Outdated mentalities, obsolete methods, and old paradigms must leave; the old attitudes must also change.

A new wineskin believer does not depend on his age but rather on his flexibility to change in mind and heart. This is because the new wine of the Holy Spirit will be poured over everyone who is thirsty enough to drink it. We should ask God to pour out His new wine in us and for us to be ready to move, to change, and to be flexible in the new move of the Holy Spirit. In Scripture, we see the new wine flow over and over again, and each time it did, it brought something powerful and significant.

What causes the new wine to come?

"16So He (Jesus) often withdrew into the wilderness and prayed." Luke 5.16

The new wine comes through prayer—lots of prayer. In the life of Jesus, prayer caused the new wine to come; the same happened when the apostles gathered together in the Upper Room. They prayed together for several days to receive the promise of the Holy Spirit.

"[1]When the Day of Pentecost had fully come, they were all with one accord[a] in one place. [2]And suddenly there came a sound from heaven, as of a rushing mighty wind, and it filled the whole house where they were sitting. [3]Then there appeared to them divided tongues, as of fire, and one sat upon each of them. [4]And they were all filled with the Holy Spirit and began to speak with other tongues, as the Spirit gave them utterance."
Acts 2.1-4

Prayer causes the powerful flow of the new wine to come into our churches, ministries, cities, and nations. Today, most people are looking for a quick-fix method that can guarantee immediate results. However, God's method for operating on earth has always been and will continue to be: the prayer of His children and their declaration of His Word. Jesus clearly showed this to us throughout His ministry in which we can see that His prayer life accomplished three very important things:

❖ It prepared the people for the coming of the new wine.

"²¹When all the people were baptized, it came to pass that Jesus also was baptized; and while He prayed, the heaven was opened." Luke 3.21

In Luke, chapter four, Jesus received the new wine after He prayed and was baptized.

"¹⁸The Spirit of the LORD is upon Me, because He has anointed Me to preach the gospel to the poor; He has sent Me to heal the brokenhearted, to proclaim liberty to the captives and recovery of sight to the blind, to set at liberty those who are oppressed; ¹⁹To proclaim the acceptable year of the LORD." Luke 4.18, 19

❖ It manifested the Kingdom of God with miracles, healings, and the rebuking of demons.

"¹⁹And the whole multitude sought to touch Him, for power went out from Him and healed them all." Luke 6.19

❖ It forced the anointing, authority, and power the disciples received.

"¹Then He called His twelve disciples together and gave them power and authority over all demons, and to cure diseases." Luke 9.1

Jesus knew He alone was not enough to carry the new wine. Furthermore, His disciples needed to begin to operate in this new area while He was still among them. That is why Jesus gave His disciples the authority to heal the sick and rebuke demons—that level of authority was made possible because of His prayer life.

What happened after Jesus and the apostles received the new wine?

Fierce opposition and persecution came against them.

"28So all those in the synagogue, when they heard these things, were filled with wrath, 29and rose up and thrust Him out of the city; and they led Him to the brow of the hill on which their city was built, that they might throw Him down over the cliff. 30Then passing through the midst of them, He went His way." Luke 4.28-30

The same happens today. When an individual accepts the apostolic reformation and the new wine, he will experience persecution and criticism from religious entities. For thirty years, Jesus kept the traditions of the Hebrew culture along with its norms and religious laws—until the new wine arrived which broke all traditions and religion without violating or altering Scripture.

Today, there are many traditions in the church that were created by men; old mentalities and methods that hinder the arrival and the flow of the new wine. Churches are spiritually dead and full of man-made programs. They operate without the power of God because of these 'old wine' traditions.

Who is called to bring the apostolic reformation?

Reformation comes through the apostles. God is raising a new generation of men through whom He is restoring the ministry of the apostle. These men are sent by Him; they have a task and a special anointing; authority, and a specific purpose that cause the flow of the new wine and a radical reformation in the spiritual, mental, economic, and governmental arenas. These men have a mentality of war and the heart of a father; they are ready and willing to raise sons in the ministry and extend the Kingdom by force.

What mayor obstacles did Jesus face when He introduced the new wine?

One might think that the strongest resistance Jesus (and apostles today) faced should have come from the unbelievers or from the people in government. However, the strongest opposition always comes from within, from the church's leadership. Jesus had to face the mayor obstacles through three types of individuals:

1. **The Pharisees.** The religious leaders that were bound to the law and Judaism were heirs to the traditions they tried to uphold; their goal

was to reach holiness through their works, but Jesus said:

"26Blind Pharisee, first cleanse the inside of the cup and dish, that the outside of them may be clean also. 27"Woe to you, scribes and Pharisees, hypocrites! For you are like whitewashed tombs which indeed appear beautiful outwardly, but inside are full of dead men's bones and all uncleanness. 28Even so you also outwardly appear righteous to men, but inside you are full of hypocrisy and lawlessness." Matthew 23.26-28

2. **The Scribes and Sadducees.** These people were the intellectual and liberals of that time. The Scribes did not believe in the supernatural; they reasoned and questioned everything trying to understand it in their minds. They did not believe in the resurrection, miracles, or rebuking demons, and that is why they persecuted Jesus to the extent that they did.

"27Then some of the Sadducees, who deny that there is a resurrection, came to Him and asked Him..." Luke 20.27

3. **The disciples of John the Baptist.** These men spoke the right words but lacked power.

"41Then many came to Him and said, "John performed no sign, but all the things that John spoke about this Man were true." John 10.41

The same obstacles that Jesus faced, which tried to stop the flow of the new wine, are still present today. Many people want to be holy by imposing their legalistic beliefs on others, such as: "You cannot use make-up," "do not drive," or "do not eat that"; these, to mention just a few. Furthermore, there are also Scribes who do not believe in the supernatural, miracles, healing, prophecy, or rebuking devils; they are so "intellectual" that they have a hard time accepting the supernatural simply because they cannot explain it through physical laws. Also, we have people who, like John's disciples, preach and teach the good Word but their lives are impoverished, in despair, and living with depression. The disciples of John the Baptist were more dangerous because they spoke the right doctrine but lived a powerless life. Like these, there are many pastors today who refer their members to psychiatrists and psychologist because they do not have the power to help them overcome their depression, mental problems, addictions, or anything else.

The Word teaches that we should know the truth, and the truth will set us free. In view of the truth that was just presented, are you a Pharisee, Scribe, or a disciple of John the Baptist? Do you think that being an old wineskin has stopped the flow of the new wine in your ministry? Are you thirsty for the new wine? Are you willing to change the way you think? Are you ready to pray for the new wine to come to your life? Are you willing and ready to be persecuted because you are a minister, believer, and leader of the apostolic new wine?

Throughout this chapter, we have learned that apostles are the new wineskins God is using to bring the apostolic reformation and the new wine. Once established, this will cause the greatest revival of the Holy Spirit ever recorded in the history of mankind.

We are living in times of reformation and the new wine; we are witnesses to the salvation of many souls, healings, and the deliverance of those who are held captive by the enemy. Furthermore, we are on the verge of seeing the destruction of old traditions, religiosity, and obsolete mentalities. We are living in new wine and new wineskin times in which people are abandoning the rigidity of their past to become flexible to the will of God and His changes. All of these things are made possible through the revelation of the Father, the end of legalism, and the free flow of the Holy Spirit.

The lifestyle of prayer led by Jesus made it possible for the apostles to flow in miracles, signs, and wonders and to change the world they lived in. Today, we have the authority that was delegated by Jesus to shake the spiritual world and cause the outpouring of the new wine; to heal and deliver those who are oppressed by the devil and to resist and overcome the violent opposition of the devil and his helpers. Legalism and intellectualism cannot remain operational when God's people begin to bring the supernatural.

2

The Calling and the Apostolic Ministry

God is restoring the ministry of the apostle, but as always, each time God restores a truth, there are individuals who take it to the extreme; this, however, does not mean it is a lie. In this case, the ministry of the apostle is being restored in the church all over the world. In some places, the ministry is fully restored and operational. In other places, it is in the process. For the purpose of clearing up any doubt and to clear the way for true apostles called by God, and with the help of the Holy Spirit, we will learn everything there is to know about the apostolic ministry. We will discover who is a true apostle; what Biblical evidence proves that an individual is an apostle and what his role is; what tools and weapons are available to him to build the Kingdom; how he builds in the Spirit using divine patterns and de-signs; what is the meaning of the apostolic spirit; what is the apostolic mentality; what an apostolic church represents for a city, the different types of apostles, their area of influence, and more.

The goal we want to achieve through this study of the ministry of the apostle is to bring the revelation of the same; to impart over those that are but who have no idea that they are; to expose those who are not; and to provide the tools that will help you differentiate between the two. In the last hundred years, God has been at work restoring the five ministerial offices. At this time, the ministries of the evangelist, teacher, pastor, and prophet are completely restored. The ministry of the apostle is the last to be in the process of restoration in the church—this has taken place within the past ten years. Once this ministry is established, the church will be complete in its capacity and training to gather the harvest of souls and to extend the Kingdom of God to the ends of the earth.

Who is an apostle?

In Greek, the word for **apostle** is *"apostolos"*; it refers to one who is sent; an ambassador, a delegate, a special messenger; a commanding officer or one who is commissioned by a higher authority.

In the New Testament, this word is used as a verb over two hundred times; it appears less times as a noun. The verb is three times more common than the noun which means that it refers more to an activity than a title. An *"apostello"* or one who is sent is what you are, not what you have. To be an apostle is more than having a title or office; it is an activity or function you live for. For instance, an individual who claims to be a licensed chauffer but does not drive is someone with a title but does not practice his role. What is the background of the verb *"apostolos* or *apostello"*? The word *apostello* is composed of two parts: *"apo"* which means one and *"stello"* which means to send. Literally, this word is defined as "one who is sent" or to order (someone) to go to an appointed place.

This verb was used by Jesus to describe the 12 men He chose to train. When they were ready, He sent them as apostles. The background of the word *"apostolos"* or one who is sent goes back to the days of Alexander the Great; he was the one who started using this word. History books teach that Alexander the Great—King of Macedonia, 350 years before Christ—would send a messenger on behalf of his kingdom or empire to accomplish a specific mission; this was his most popular method used to conquer other nations.

The commander of this special force was called an *"apostolos"*; the king would give him the power and authority to establish the Greek empire wherever he was sent. This was called an apostolic mission, and the soldiers were referred to as the apostolic team. This team would arrive at the appointed place, fight against the enemy, destroy it, and finally establish a base of operation to govern the nation in the name of Alexander the Great. The word *"apostolos"* describes the leader of a special group of individuals who were sent with the authority and specific purpose of conquering a territory for the king, and establish his kingdom.

In other words, this is a strictly military term. This elite force was composed by a small group of individuals who were well trained and equipped for war; they were the first to take over a small portion of the enemy's territory; the first to lead the way and establish the kingdom for Alexander the Great.

What is an elite force?[1]

An elite force is a minority group of people who meet the requirements and special unique skills and characteristics within their field of service. In the United States armed forces, there are special elite forces like the Rangers—elite troops specialized in attack and destroy missions. These forces are trained to conquer and destroy the most difficult objectives either by land, air, or sea anywhere in the world and at any time. Rangers work in teams of twelve; these men establish a special friendship of loyalty and trust for life. They are trained to handle all types of situations—each knowing each other's specialty. To them, the mission is a priority and nothing distracts them from their objective. They are so skilled that two rangers trained as sharp-shooters can hold captive an entire company of two hundred men. Two fundamental values for these soldiers are: the mission

---

[1] Hughes, Jimmy. Special Elite Force (information taken from his experience as a ranger when he joined the military in 1975).

and taking care of the other team members' life; hence, the reason why they are taught not to leave a man behind. If a ranger is wounded on a mission and is unable to continue, he must stay put, hide, and wait until the rest of the team can return safely to find him. However, if the enemy is nearby, he must fight back the enemy and give up his life if necessary to protect the rest of the team. His comrades will mark the place on the map where he was last seen so they can return later to collect his body. Their logo is: no man, dead or alive, is left behind on enemy territory.

The missions of this elite group include the search and rescue of people who are under attack, oppression, tortured, or held against their will. Does not this sound the same as the mission that Jesus left the church? The church should have the same attitude in its daily walk with Christ, as a ranger has on a regular workday. The apostolic team is like a team of rangers; it has a specific mission; it carries special weapons; it is trained to take on missions that ordinary men are unable or untrained to handle, and its members must be loyal and committed one to the other. The church should learn from the rangers to live in constant training. Rangers learn to fight, fast, and deal with any type of situation and pain like no other men can; this should be the attitude of the body of Christ.

By the time Jesus trained and taught His disciples—His elite force—the word 'apostle' and the apostolic idea had already been established. Jesus took the first twelve, and after He called and trained them for war against the enemy, He gave them weapons of warfare and rules to live by with the other disciples; after giving them strategies for war, He commissioned them to be apostles.

"14Then He appointed twelve, that they might be with Him and that He might send them out to preach." Mark 3.14

What mission did Jesus have as an apostle of God?

Over and over again, Jesus declared that He had been sent by the Father; He was an apostle on a mission from the Father to establish His Kingdom on earth.

"43...but He said to them, "I must preach the kingdom of God to the other cities also, because for this purpose I have been sent." Luke 4.43

His mission was to announce and establish the Kingdom of God throughout the world. Just as Jesus was sent, He sends us to do the same thing He did. In other words, every believer has an apostolic mission to fulfill. This, however, does not mean that every believer is an apostle.

"21So Jesus said to them again, "Peace to you! As the Father has sent Me, I also send you." John 20.21

To sum up, an apostle is one who is sent by Jesus on an expedition to conquer and establish His name and Kingdom in the enemy's territory. Therefore, to be an apostle or to be a part of an apostolic team is a military role or responsibility. An apostle is not just an individual who travels; he is someone who travels with purpose and a specific mission in mind. Therefore, a person cannot call himself an apostle unless the king commissions him as such. In my case, Jesus commissioned me to be an apostle. He gave me a specific mission and an apostolic team with a heart ready for war; together, we will carry out the apostolic mission.

My Personal Testimony

How did God call me to be an apostle?

Before I answer this question, it is necessary to establish the fact that apostles are elected, chosen, commissioned, and sent by Jesus, not by men or committees.

"11...He Himself gave some to be apostles..."
Ephesians 4.11

Jesus is the One who calls, commissions, constitutes, and sends His disciples; they are the building materials needed to build His church.

Jesus does not delegate this responsibility to anyone; He does it himself. Today, there are many who call themselves apostles; they commissioned themselves, but the signs of a true apostle do not follow them. They take advantage of the people who are less knowledgeable and whose heart is pure. Their actions shame the gospel of Christ. It is for this reason that many people are skeptical or refuse to have anything to do with the apostolic movement; they think it is all a farce—even true apostles refuse to associate themselves with the apostolic movement out fear of being judged by the people and compared or associated with those who are not. However, these people should understand—their eyes should be opened—that there are many true apostles who love God and His people; they are apostles who were genuinely sent by Jesus to build and edify the body of Christ. These men are a blessing for God's people because they do not follow personal agendas—their divine agenda is to edify the Kingdom and the church.

How does God commission a man to be an apostle?

The apostolic calling is a personal one in which God speaks directly into our spirit through different means: His Word, the inner witness, prophecies, dreams, a personal visitation from God, or any other way God might choose.

Afterwards, this calling is confirmed by men of great spiritual maturity—apostles who have been in the ministry for a long time, whose fruits are abundant, and who have a great testimony. These men are sent to validate the calling that is in us.

Not all believers in the body of Christ are called to be apostles; only a few are chosen by God to carry out this task. For instance, the apostle Paul—Jesus separated and commissioned him to be an apostle. Paul received the revelation of his ministry in Damascus, and after 14 years, he went to Jerusalem where he found the other disciples who validated his ministry.

"1Then, after fourteen years, I went up again to Jerusalem with Barnabas and also took Titus with me. 2And I went up by revelation, and communicated to them that gospel which I preach among the Gentiles, but privately to those who were of reputation, lest by any means I might run, or had run, in vain."
Galatians 2.1, 2

Paul was commissioned by Jesus, but he still waited for the other apostles to validate his ministry and the revelation he had received directly from God; he did this because he was in submission to the other apostles. Today, there are many 'apostles' who answer to no one; they do what they want, how they want it, and in the end, they abuse their position and the people.

What is an apostle of Jesus sent to do?

Throughout Scripture, we find that to be sent by God, as an apostle, has five specific assignations:

1. **The apostle is sent with a specific purpose.**

   Jesus was sent by the Father to establish His Kingdom and announce the good news of the gospel.

   "43...but He said to them, "I must preach the kingdom of God to the other cities also, because for this purpose I have been sent." Luke 4.43

   Jesus did not come to make himself famous, to create a business, or to boast about himself. He came with a pre-established assignment to accomplish. God is precise; Therefore, He does not experiment because He already has something specific for each of us to do. Of course, Jesus came to die for the sins of humanity, and as part of His mission, He took away our infirmities and sickness. However, He had a specific purpose which He carried out completely.

2. **The apostle is sent to carry out a specific task.**

   When Alexander the Great would send an apostle with an apostolic team, he would assign them a specific mission or task along with the authority to execute it. The word

THE CALLING AND THE APOSTOLIC MINISTRY

"mission" is defined as a commission that is given by a state or king, in this case, to a diplomat or special agent to accomplish a particular assignment.

"⁸He who does what is sinful is of the devil, because the devil has been sinning from the beginning. The reason the Son of God appeared was to destroy the devil's work." 1 John 3.8

The apostolic ministry has to do with accomplishing missions for our King—Jesus; these are specific, exact, and precise; they have one goal: to establish and extend His Kingdom. The ministry of the apostle is characterized by the precision with which the work of the Lord is done. What mission has God entrusted you to do? Are you an ambassador of the Kingdom and of Jesus? Are you ready to accomplish the military mission and destroy the kingdom of darkness?

Many apostles today are unaware of the purpose or mission the King sent them to do; hence, the reason why they work on different projects but nothing specific. They speak in general about plans and purposes but not about something in particular or in detail.

Illustration: I do not have the specific mission from God to help the poor and build orphanages around the world, but in the ministry, we take time to serve our community in this area. We have established orphanages, and we help those who are financially in need. However, that is not my specific mission. My mission is to raise men and women and help them find their calling and purpose in God; to train, equip, and send them to do the work of the ministry and extend the Kingdom. We help the poor because it is Biblical to do it and also because God commands every believer to practice it, but our goals, efforts, and resources are projected towards the mission that God sent us to do.

3. **The apostle is sent with a specific vision of what he should do.**

Many people follow the vision of other men because they do not know their own. However, when God gives a vision, it is specific, detailed, and made to fit the person who obeys it.

The vision is the plan and will of God for your life; it is God's dream for you to accomplish it during your stay on earth. God will not give you something that is general or uncertain in nature. He will give you something concrete; a specific vision that will attract certain type of people to your ministry. What is your vision? Have you written down your vision?

4. The apostle is sent to a specific place.

"16You have not chosen Me, but I have chosen you and I have appointed you [I have planted you], that you might go and bear fruit and keep on bearing, and that your fruit may be lasting [that it may remain, abide], so that whatever you ask the Father in My Name [as presenting all that I AM], He may give it to you." John 15.16

The expression *"I have planted you"* means: to place in a specific location and to relate with specific people. God places the apostle in a place where he will have a circle or sphere of influence that has been predetermined and set by God—this is because the apostle will only be effective when he is with the right people in the right place. The end-result of being in a specific place, with the people God sent him to be with, is that the apostle will bear abundant fruit. If there is no fruit, that is a sign that he is not in the right place or with the right people.

5. The apostle is sent with a specific authority.

The word **authority**, in Greek, is the word *"exousia"*; it means to grant legal rights to use power, authority, right, liberty, jurisdiction, or strength.

If an apostle does not have the authority given by God and his spiritual covering, he will not have the power to carry out the mission and vision because, without that authority, he does not have the legal right to accomplish them. More than likely, an apostle without power is one who sent himself, and that is why he has no support. Jesus sent His disciples with the authority to rebuke demons, heal the sick, and preach the gospel; they obeyed Jesus and were very successful.

"[1]...and when He had called His twelve disciples to Him, He gave them power over unclean spirits, to cast them out, and to heal all kinds of sickness and all kinds of disease." Matthew 10.1

The apostle is sent to a specific place with five particular assignations: purpose, mission, vision, a place, and authority. This is the only way to fully operate in the apostolic anointing and know that God's support is backing us up.

When God sends an apostle, prophet, pastor, teacher, or evangelist, he should be welcomed as such.

Apostles are only able to operate in their anointing when they establish a relationship; it is not enough to recognize them as such. Apostles and the apostolic anointing are fully operational where they are sent by the Lord and where they are welcomed and recognized as such—that is the only way they can exercise their paternity.

To fully receive the benefits that accompany an apostle, he has to be accepted and welcomed as such.

"⁴⁰He who receives you receives Me, and he who receives Me receives Him who sent Me. ⁴¹He who receives a prophet in the name of a prophet shall receive a prophet's reward. And he who receives a righteous man in the name of a righteous man shall receive a righteous man's reward."
Matthew 10.40, 41

What is the reward of a prophet?

The reward of a prophet is to receive the benefits of grace, favor, and the anointing in which he operates. Why? Because when the gift is welcomed, the person is also welcomed along with the giver of the gift—Jesus—that is why there is a reward.

*"⁸Therefore He says: "When He ascended on high, He led captivity captive, and **gave gifts to men."***
Ephesians 4.8

What is the reward for receiving an apostle?

The grace, favor, and the anointing that operate in him will be imparted on the one who welcomes the apostle, his gifts, and the one who sent him.

Illustration: In my experience, some ministries only welcomed the gift of teaching or preaching which limited me to only those two areas. I cannot fully operate as an apostle in a church that only welcomes me as a teacher.

To receive the full benefits of the apostolic ministry, you have to willingly recognize him, give him the authority and honor in the church, and welcome him, as Jesus said. If not, you will not be able to see the powerful manifestation of the apostolic ministry. If you welcome a teacher, you will have the reward of a teacher; if you welcome a prophet, you will have the reward of a prophet; if you welcome a pastor, you will have the reward of a pastor, and so on.

Illustration: The apostle Paul spent three years in the church at Corinth, but the believers never recognized him as an apostle; quite the opposite—they accused him of not being one. That is why the church at Corinth never became powerful. However, the same apostle spent three years in Thessalonica where he was welcomed as such; that church became very powerful and with less members than the church at Corinth; they preached the gospel they heard from Paul and impacted thousands of people in the area with the power of God. This was made possible because Paul was able to influence them with his apostolic ministry; they accepted and welcomed him as an apostle; they respected and honored him, and in return, they received their reward.

"13For this reason we also thank God without ceasing, because when you received the word of God which you heard from us, you welcomed it not as the word of men, but as it is in truth, the word of God, which also effectively works in you who believe." 1 Thessalonians 2.13

Why did God send me as an apostle?

What is my mission and purpose? What is my vision and with what authority do I operate in? What is the specific place God has sent me to? My calling is apostolic at the local and global level. God sent me with a specific authority to carry out a specific mission which is to reach the ten percent of the population in the city of Miami for Christ. The purpose in my life is to establish the Kingdom of God in this city, in the United States, and in the rest of the world with the specific vision to evangelize, affirm, disciple, and send men and women to do the work of the Lord; to commission every leader and disciple to do the will of the Father and to reach their destiny, and in doing so, to take the

Kingdom everywhere they go. Also, to send leaders equipped with powerful weapons useful to extend the Kingdom of God by force by rebuking the devil, healing the sick, and performing signs, miracles, and wonders; by raising the dead, preaching, teaching, and prophesizing the mysteries of the Kingdom and to cause a reformation and an impact on society. I have been sent to do these things in order to accomplish the ultimate goal which is to transfer the legacy of blessing, prosperity, and justice to future generations.

How did God call me into the apostolic ministry?

Years after my salvation, I received the call in my Spirit; I knew it had come from God. I always knew that my call was not an ordinary one; I felt it in my spirit. God confirmed my calling through dreams, and I received the vision in prayer; also, my call was confirmed through numerous prophetic words and many men of great spiritual maturity.

The Validation and Confirmation of the Apostolic Ministry in My Life

Years ago, Ronald Short, my spiritual father, came to visit me. He said that God had awakened him early one morning and given him the detailed description of the apostolic calling that was on my life. Ronald Short is an apostle with over forty years of experience in the ministry; a man with great knowledge, integrity, and personal testimony; he is also an apostle to the Hispanic people—he was my mentor for many years. By his side, I learned to love the people, to move in the gifts of the Holy Spirit, and above all, he taught me the meaning of humbleness. In his apostolic ministry, the signs of an apostle such as patience, signs, wonders, miracles, healing, raising the dead, and more, followed him.

When the apostle Ronald Short described what God had shown him about me, I could not accept it because, according to my under-standing at that time, to be an apostle meant nothing more than having a title. My unbelief was also fueled by the fact that I had seen more than my share of false apostles, and I did not want to be associated with them. After him came the apostle and prophet Bill Hamon—he has over fifty years of ministerial experience and is one of the founders and pioneers of the restoration of the prophetic ministry around the world. Ronald Short also activated thousands of men and women in this area with his integrity, transparency, and good testimony. The Apostle Hamon was the second to confirm the apostolic ministry in my life and trained me in the prophetic area of my ministry. Today, he is my spiritual father and spiritual authority.

After him, apostles and prophets of such stature as John Eckhardt, Peter Wagner, Cindy Jacobs, Cathy Lechner, Kingsley Fletcher, Tommy Tenney, Chuck Pierce, Kim Clement, Hank Kunneman, Alan Vincent, and many more confirmed and validated my apostolic ministry. In short, it took me almost two years to receive and accept this new role. By then, I had finally realized that being an apostle was not a title but a role—another important thing I learned was that, to operate under the anointing of that ministry, one has to accept the ministry. If the commission is not accepted, neither the authority nor the power can be conferred by the King to the apostle—the one who is sent. How do I prove that I am an apostle? The answer is easy. Look at the fruit of our ministry and you will have your answer.

I should emphasize the fact that I did not start the ministry being an apostle. My first ministry was to serve in different departments at church. I served as an usher, deacon, elder, and I did one-on-one evangelism. I was a Sunday school teacher and more. After many years of service, I was ordained as a minister in the local church. After this, I started to travel to the nations as an evangelist and teacher of the

Word; preaching in massive crusades to win souls for the Kingdom and teaching in seminars and churches. After nine years as an evangelist, God called me to be a pastor. I was a successful pastor of a local church where I also started to flow in the prophetic ministry—the prophetic has been a gift that I use only when a specific situation required the prophetic word to be spoken.

Twelve years later, after successfully serving in the ministries mentioned, God called me into the apostolic ministry. He has confirmed His call, over and over again, through the abundant fruits, signs, wonders, and miracles; through the many churches that were planted, the churches and ministries that were adopted and are now under our spiritual covering, and with the mega church that we now have which touches the lives of thousands of sons and daughters that are being trained for the ministry in the different parts of Miami and Latin America.

In conclusion, we can say that an apostle is one who is sent by God; a delegate, messenger, military officer; the leader of an elite group with the mission to conquer a territory for his King.

The first official apostle in the Bible is Jesus. He was sent by God, the Father, clothed with divine grace, the full armor, and equipped with all the gifts of the Holy Spirit. Jesus was sent with a specific purpose, a precise mission, to a definite place, with a detailed vision, and unwavering authority. God empowered Him with these things to help Him carry out the job He was sent to do. Jesus established the Kingdom of God, restored the relationship between the Heavenly Father and mankind, and recovered the power and authority the devil had stolen from mankind.

When the mission was completed, Jesus delegated his anointing and authority to the apostles whom He had formed and trained during His ministry and to Paul on his way to Damascus. He did this so they would continue His work in future generations — that was His inheritance.

Jesus is the only One who calls and commissions apostles on earth; He does it the same way the Father did with him. Jesus sends an apostle to a specific place, with a mission, vision, purpose, and specific authority, and later, other apostles, prophets, and ministries confirm that calling.

An apostle is unable to accomplish his vision unless he has the specific authority given by God to do it.

3

Biblical Signs
that Follow an Apostle

There is much confusion about the apostolic ministry because the church does not recognize the Biblical signs that follow this type of ministry; these signs prove the authenticity of the apostle. They reveal his integrity and inner and exterior nature as a man. Therefore, these signs are not the functions he carries out but the revelation of what the man really is: his fruit, character, attitude, heart, and wisdom; his relationship with God, authority in the Spirit, his works, and deeds.

"²This man came to Jesus by night and said to Him, "Rabbi, we know that You are a teacher come from God; for no one can do these signs that You do unless God is with him." John 3.2

No one can perform signs and wonders unless God backs him up; these demonstrate that God is with him.

Signs and wonders cannot be fabricated, produced, or invented with human strength; they are the result of the power and approval that God gives to a man. Biblical signs are the evidence, seal of authenticity, and guarantee of quality of an apostle.

What is a sign?

In Greek, the word for **sign** is *"semeion"*; it means sign, miracle, wonder, or token; that which distinguishes one person from the next.

"12Truly the signs of an apostle were accomplished among you with all perseverance, in signs and wonders and mighty deeds." 2 Corinthians 12.12

Paul mentions a few of the signs that are, in truth, the most important in the life of a genuine apostle. However, we find in the Word more signs which describe who and what an apostle is; these signs make up the pattern of the life of all apostles because they are common to each of them.

What important Biblical signs follow a genuine apostle?

The best way to find out about a person, gift, or ministry is to create a profile or picture of it; it is basically the same method used to recognize counterfeit money among the genuine article. There are many signs, but in this chapter, only the most important will be mentioned. I have seen this in my life and in the lives of many other genuine apostles.

1. The apostle can only be appointed by our Lord Jesus Christ.

"¹¹And He Himself gave some to be apostles, some prophets, some evangelists, and some pastors and teachers." Ephesians 4.11

The calling of an apostle is the end result of a supernatural revelation received while in intimacy with Jesus—in a direct encounter with Him in the Spirit. It is an assignation personally given by the Lord directly into the one being called. This revelation can come through dreams, visions, the Word, a personal visitation from Jesus, the prophetic word, or any other way He might choose; either way, it will be a method that will leave no room for doubt. This personal and direct revelation from God is later confirmed by other reputable apostles and prophets within the body of Christ; they will make that calling official before the people and the church.

Apostles cannot be commissioned by councils or committees, only by Jesus. After the calling is received, the only job for men to do is to commission the apostle in public and confirm what Jesus already did in the Spirit. To be separated, chosen, commissioned, and elected to be an apostle, directly by God, helps us to stand firm and steady through even the worse opposition and persecution. On the other hand, it is impossible for an individual, who chose to commission himself, to have the grace and the authority to face the enemy's oppression and persecution.

What is the difference between being called and being commissioned?[2]

Many individuals were called by our Lord and immediately started to serve in the ministry, but this is not the right way to do it. The Bible teaches there is a process everyone must endure between the time one is called and the time one is sent. Of course, God could do it a different way, but that would be the exception to the rule.

"[16]...So the last will be first, and the first last. For many are called, but few chosen." Matthew 20.16

Another way to read this verse would be: "Many are called, but few are commissioned." This process took 17 years for David, 15 years for Paul, and 12 years for me to endure, and so on. In the process one must endure between the time one is called and the time one is commissioned, there are two extremes:

❖ To be called and begin to serve without undergoing the process. This extreme causes

---

[2] Hamon, Bill Dr. *Apostles, Prophets and the Coming Moves of God.* Destiny Image Publishers, Inc., 1997, ISBN: 0-939868-09-1.

many people to fail in their ministry because they are not ready in character or as ministers.

❖ To be called and never sent. These people were called to serve but never prepared for it; they disobeyed the Lord, and that is why they were never commissioned.

The method God uses is: first, He calls; second, one must endure the training process; and third, one is commissioned. Jesus calls and commissions an apostle. He gives the apostle specific mission, a set vision, a sphere of influence, purpose, the authority to govern, and the power that will back him up. Usually, a man does not start as an apostle from the beginning. First, he must serve in the different ministerial offices of Ephesians 4.11—pastor, evangelist, prophet, or teacher.

2. Apostles have the divine grace to patiently endure and persevere to build.

"12Truly the signs of an apostle were accomplished among you with all perseverance, in signs and wonders and mighty deeds..." 2 Corinthians 12.12

Patience is a very important sign in the character of an apostle. Paul mentions it several times throughout his writings.

Apostolic patience covers the following three areas:

❖ The apostolic patience to build

In Greek, the word for **patience** is *"hupomone"*; it refers to the ability to endure trials and tribulations for long periods of time; to be encouraged and not lose one's peace even when undergoing intense pressure; a long-lasting and joyful resistance.

It is not enough to endure persecution if the expression on our faces is one of misery which seeks the compassion of others. Patience means to endure the test joyfully, and this joy should be obvious in our facial expression because persecution should never lead us to a state of desperation. The apostle has that grace which comes from God; that is why he is able to build, though it might take long periods of time, without feeling desperate or discouraged.

"[3]...and not only that, but we also glory in tribulations, knowing that tribulation produces perseverance; [4] and perseverance, character; and character, hope." Romans 5.3, 4

What Paul said was that he had the grace to glory in tribulation, which produced or exercised his patience to persevere, which in turn built his character that led to hope.

In the previous verse, it says that perseverance produces character; in actuality, it means that the person's character is tested by undergoing great pressure, persecution, and crisis for long periods of time. Without this virtue, the apostle is unable to continue or persevere in his calling because the difficulties he will encounter in life will be many and constant.

Apostles are characterized by the grace they have to build, with patience, in future generations and for long periods of time. They do not look for short cuts or easy methods when dealing with the unexpected inconveniences. Rather, they build with care and dedication because their mind-set is multi-generational.

For instance, prophets have the ability to see something in the spirit but not the patience to build it. Apostles, on the other hand, have the grace to build and persevere to the end even if the circumstances are less than optimal, full of pressure, and persecution. The apostle can build in prayer, doctrine, grace, and in the calling; he can build in faith, the taking over of a city, in the training of leaders, and in establishing divine plans on earth. He can endure persecution and trials without feeling discouraged and without losing his drive.

❖ **Perseverance to build for future generations**

"42And they continued steadfastly in the apostles' doctrine and fellowship, in the breaking of bread, and in prayers." Acts 2.42

Another sign that goes with patience is apostolic perseverance; once an apostle sees something, he is like a pit bull that seizes his target and does not let go until something happens. Apostles have the grace to hold on to a project or vision until it is carried through to completion. They see the future and persevere in what they see until it is completed.

We are not going to take the city overnight, in two years, or three, but if we persevere, persist, and work hard, we will reach our goal. The apostle's perseverance is so strong that if he is unable to reach his goals, he will train others to accomplish it in the future. You will find that everything an apostle begins he finishes and does it well because God has given him the grace to persevere in everything He calls him to do and shows His support by giving him of His power and provision.

❖ **The grace to suffer for His name's sake and for the Kingdom**

The nature of the apostolic ministry requires the grace to suffer because the apostle is the individual that paves the way for others. Because of the revelations he receives, the apostle is the first to go forward, and this fuels the enemy's anger against him; hence, the reason why Jesus declared the following:

"⁴⁹Therefore the wisdom of God also said, 'I will send them prophets and apostles, and some of them they will kill and persecute." Luke 11.49

When the Lord called Paul, He spoke about the suffering he would have to endure for His name sake.

"¹⁶For I will show him how many things he must suffer for My name's sake." Acts 9.16

This word came to pass in the life of Paul. As a matter of fact, years later, we read a list of afflictions he had to endure when the believers in Corinth rejected him as one called to be an apostle.

"23Are they ministers of Christ?—I speak as a fool—I am more: in labors more abundant, in stripes above measure, in prisons more frequently, in deaths often. 24From the Jews five times I received forty stripes minus one. 25Three times I was beaten with rods; once I was stoned; three times I was shipwrecked; a night and a day I have been in the deep; 26in journeys often, in perils of waters, in perils of robbers, in perils of my own countrymen, in perils of the Gentiles, in perils in the city, in perils in the wilderness, in perils in the sea, in perils among false brethren; 27in weariness and toil, in sleeplessness often, in hunger and thirst, in fastings often, in cold and nakedness—."
2 Corinthians 11.23-27

However, as bad as these afflictions were, they were not the worse to endure. I say this because if we continue reading, we find that the betrayal and abandonment of his spiritual children and of some of the members of his apostolic team was the hardest and most painful to endure.

"16At my first defense no one stood with me, but all forsook me. May it not be charged against them." 2 Timothy 4.16

The apostle who wrote 14 books of the New Testament was alone—everyone abandoned him. Who would ever imagine such a thing could be possible?

"⁹Be diligent to come to me quickly; ¹⁰for Demas has forsaken me, having loved this present world, and has departed for Thessalonica—Crescens for Galatia, Titus for Dalmatia." 2 Timothy 4.9, 10

Demas was one of Paul's disciples who betrayed and abandoned him when he disagreed with Paul; this caused great pain in Paul who was only able to overcome by the grace given to him by God.

As an apostle, I fully understand what Paul was talking about. A few of my spiritual children—after I was the channel used by God to restore and edify them—betrayed me, not because of anything I did but because a spirit of betrayal entered their lives. Apostles can endure without losing their mind or sensitivity, and still continue in the edification of spiritual children, only because of the grace given by God to overcome the betrayal and pain caused by the abandonment of those children they worked so hard to raise. I think it is a crazy endeavor to try and exercise the position of an apostle without the grace of God to cushion the pain that accompanies this office.

Why does God give apostles the grace to suffer?

→ To comfort and console others.

> *"⁴...who comforts us in all our tribulation, that we may be able to comfort those who are in any trouble, with the comfort with which we ourselves are comforted by God."*
> *2 Corinthians 1.4*

→ To allow the life of Christ to manifest through them.

> *"¹¹...that the life of Jesus also may be manifested in our mortal flesh."*
> *2 Corinthians 4.11*

3. Apostles have the heart of a father.

Apostles become the founding fathers of churches and spiritual children; they also adopt churches, ministries, and children who are without a spiritual father. This is an important sign in an apostle because their greatest passion should be to raise natural and spiritual children and help them recognize their calling in God. The greatest gift of an apostle is the ability to impart and teach other leaders the revelation he has received through a paternal relationship—his teaching method is through discipleship.

4. Apostles are wise master builders of the Kingdom of God.

   "10According to the grace of God which was given to me, as a wise master builder I have laid the foundation, and another builds on it. But let each one take heed how he builds on it."
   1 Corinthians 3.10

   A master builder is one who is learned, experienced, capable, and trained in a science or art; he designs the plan for buildings to be constructed. In the Kingdom of God, apostles are the designers or architects. They are passionate when it comes to building powerful ministries, churches, or nations according to Biblical standard. Apostles are not satisfied with simply building a church or ministry; their greatest satisfaction comes when they build and extend the Kingdom of God and the church. They know how to do it because God shows them the master plan and equips them in special ways to carry it out.

5. Apostles proclaim and demonstrate the Word with miracles, healing, signs, and wonders.

   "4And my speech and my preaching were not with persuasive words of human wisdom, but in demons-

tration of the Spirit and of power, [5]that your faith should not be in the wisdom of men but in the power of God." 1 Corinthians 2.4, 5

The Word and the work of our hands go together. Wherever an apostle shares the gospel, the Word is confirmed with miracles, healing, prophesy, the expulsion of demons, and more. The powerful manifestation of the Spirit and power of God is evident in the life of an apostle; this is because without the demonstration of God's power, people's faith would only be based on human knowledge and wisdom. This is not what God wants nor does it align with the mission to edify because without signs, the apostle cannot build the Kingdom in people's lives.

6. The fruit in the ministry of the apostle is obvious and abundant.

"[2]If I am not an apostle to others, yet doubtless I am to you. For you are the seal of my apostleship in the Lord." 1 Corinthians 9.2

Apostles produce great ministerial results. For instance:

❖ The edification of churches in the city; regional centers where the ministerial offices found in Ephesians 4.11 are trained.

80

❖ The establishment of churches full of power that multiply quickly and which exert great influence in the city.

❖ The reproduction and development of spiritual children who, when sent, serve the Lord successfully. The Apostle Paul said that the reproduction of spiritual children was the seal of an apostleship.

❖ They write books and teach new revelations that edify the church. Apostles receive a lot of revelation from God, and because of it, it is important to register it in books, manuals, and teaching material to make it easy to impart it to the thousands that spiritually feed from it.

❖ The influence of the apostolic authority in the city. The true apostle touches the lives of politicians, presidents, government leaders, senators, mayors, and business people with the grace God gives him. These people seek the advice of the apostle because they recognize the divine wisdom in their lives.

❖ They are able to influence the media, education, and the construction of buildings; in the buying of land, the economy, business, the judicial system, and more. This apostolic mark is made possible because of the grace found in the apostle to be a pioneer, to be first, to pave the way for new things to happen—things that have not taken place before.

❖ The respect, admiration, and honor from his natural children and spouse. The true apostle bears abundant fruit and is consistent with his immediate family.

7. The mature apostle has experience in the five-fold ministerial offices.

As mentioned earlier, no one can exercise the office of apostle until he endures the process which implies time and growth. All men who are now operating within the apostolic ministry are men who started their service in one of the other Ephesians 4.11 ministries.

When they matured, they started to operate in the five ministries—this is an apostolic sign.

If you doubt the authenticity of the ministry of an apostle, ask yourself the following questions:

• How many strong churches has this man established in the city?

• How many ministers has he trained for the Ephesians 4.11 offices?

- How many spiritual children has he raised and led to discover their calling?

- How much influence does he have over politicians, authorities, and business men in the city?

- How many things has he accomplished that other men have been unable to do?

- Has he advanced the Kingdom in the political arena, the business sector, the educational and judicial systems, or in the media?

- How many books has he written? What new revelations of God's Word has he taught the church?

- Has he operated in all the ministerial offices found in Ephesians 4.11 before becoming an apostle?

Today, many call themselves apostles but they have no fruits or evidence in any of these areas to support their claim. Jesus said that we would recognize them by their fruit!

8. Apostles receive abundant revelation from God.

"⁷And lest I should be exalted above measure by the abundance of the revelations, a thorn in the flesh

was given to me, a messenger of Satan to buffet me, lest I be exalted above measure." 2 Corinthians 12.7

Most of the Bible was written by apostles and prophets because God chose these two ministries to reveal the mysteries which produce four things in believers:

❖ **Activation:** it activates the spiritual gifts that lay dormant in people.

> *"⁶Therefore I remind you to stir up the gift of God which is in you through the laying on of my hands." 2 Timothy 1.6*

❖ **Impartation:** the transference of virtues and gifts into believers that produce a spiritual quickening in their lives and which leads them to maturity.

> *"¹¹For I long to see you, that I may impart to you some spiritual gift, so that you may be established." Romans 1.11*

❖ **Demonstration:** this visually or physically demonstrates the supernatural power of God.

> *"⁴And my speech and my preaching were not with persuasive words of human wisdom, but in demonstration of the Spirit and of power, ⁵that*

your faith should not be in the wisdom of men but in the power of God." 1 Corinthians 2.4, 5

❖ **Transformation:** the end result of a revelation is the total transformation of the believer—as it happened to Simon. The influence exerted by Jesus changed Paul; he went from being a weak reed to a building block.

9. Apostles have governmental authority.

Apostles are known for their great level of authority over the people, leaders, cities, and nations and for their special authority to destroy principalities and strongholds. The apostle receives from God, the governmental authority to do two things:

- To represent Jesus and His Kingdom as an ambassador for Christ.

- To take charge and govern in the spiritual realm.

The authority to govern is one of the strongest signs that a man is an apostle. He can exercise his authority to establish a decree against sin and the enemy; also, to discipline, correct, and edify the people. This authority is for the edification of the church and not for its destruction.

A man who is genuinely called to be an apostle will use his authority to unite the leaders and the people in order to win the city; also, to discipline those who are living a sinful lifestyle. The authority to govern is a powerful spiritual punch against the kingdom of darkness. Sometimes, that authority is intimidating because of its determining impact of power; hence, the reason why the apostle operates in humility is because he understands that he was chosen to serve the people, not to manipulate or control them.

Illustration: In 2005, we experienced the menacing power of two hurricanes that were determined to come against Miami; hurricane Katrina in September and Wilma in October.

In view of their impending arrival, as an apostle and together with the people, I raised a decree ordering the hurricanes to change their course away from our city. A few hours later, we praised God because the hurricanes did change their course enough to cause little or no damage to our area.

10. Apostles are powerful, courageous, spiritual warriors.

"⁴For the weapons of our warfare are not carnal but mighty in God for pulling down strongholds." 2 Corintios 10.4

Apostles receive the designs and strategies to do warfare against the enemy; they are the governors of the Kingdom of God and a terror to the kingdom of darkness. They take charge when it comes to conquering cities and new territories. In the previous verse, Paul speaks in terms that are strictly military, and according to what we have learned so far, even the name "apostle" has to do with warfare.

11. Apostles have reached a high level of spiritual maturity.

"13...till we all come to the unity of the faith and of the knowledge of the Son of God, to a perfect man, to the measure of the stature of the fullness of Christ." Ephesians 4.13

The character and life of Jesus are evident in an apostle; these manifest in the way they speak, think, and act; in their humility, integrity, and fear of the Lord; in the way they lead their families, how they handle their finances, and in their moral behavior, attitudes, and motivations. Many people want to imitate the character of an apostle, not only because of the gifts they possess but also because they model the life of Jesus.

"16Therefore I urge you, imitate me. 17For this reason, I have sent Timothy to you, who is my

beloved and faithful son in the Lord, who will remind you of my ways in Christ, as I teach everywhere in every church."
1 Corinthians 4.16, 17

The strongest sign of an apostle is that they reflect the character of Jesus in their joy, kindness, humility, and service.

For a brief review, let us say that apostles are teachers and builders of the Kingdom; they have divine wisdom and they demonstrate the visible power of God in the miracles, signs, and wonders they perform. That is why the ministry of the true apostle bears noticeable and abundant fruit. They have the grace given by God to persevere where others have given up; to suffer what others have been unable to endure and to be patient when others are driven to despair.

The call of the apostle comes directly from Jesus who equips him with the grace, patience, and composure needed to carry out the mission. He is also equipped with the ability to overcome the opposition from the enemy, the doubters, and from the people who are still under the influence of the old wine mentality. This grace also empowers the apostle with the ability to invest himself in others with his gifts, wisdom, and abilities to shape the apostolic leaders of tomorrow.

Apostles model the character of Jesus because they are full of His divine love to rescue the lost; also, because they are strong worriers against Satan and his demons.

4

Essential Roles or Functions of an Apostle

4

Essential Roles or Functions of an Apostle

I n today's society, many call themselves apostles, but in truth, what they have is a title or position not a calling because they do not function as such. To be an apostle is much more than having a title; it means to operate in the different areas in which he is called to serve and to bear abundant fruit in each of them. In this chapter, we will expand on the role or function of a genuine apostle and the different spheres of influence that are assigned to him.

What is a role or function?

A role or function is a responsibility; an activity that relates to a charge or calling; it is what an individual does continuously—the role is what one does not the title one carries. Apostles have the ability to flow in such roles when they operate in:

❖ The right sphere of influence to which they were assigned.

❖ The specific place where they were sent.

❖ The place where they are welcomed and accepted as such.

❖ The place where their paternal role is recognized and accepted.

❖ The specific mission they were entrusted to carry out.

❖ The specific vision they received.

❖ The specific authority that was given to them.

When these are carried out, the church or ministry receive the benefits of the apostolic anointing; the establishment of the Kingdom accelerates, and their work becomes more precise. When these are in order, it means the apostle is operating in the fullness of his calling and the people are blessed, edified, trained, and society is touched by the power of God.

What are the essential roles of an apostle who is sent by Jesus?

1. **An apostle is a spiritual father who conceives, births, and adopts spiritual children.**

"15For though you might have ten thousand instructors in Christ, yet you do not have many fathers; for in Christ Jesus I have begotten you through the gospel." 1 Corinthians 4.15

The apostle is called to be a father to God's people; his primary responsibility is to raise children; to serve, help them identify their gifts, discover their purpose, and help them carry out their mission. The fundamental apostolic role is to be a good father; one who encourages, strengthens, and disciplines his spiritual children. His great passion is to see his children grow and mature in the ministry until they are able to depend completely on God; to carry out His purpose and will and someday be commissioned to do the same: to become fathers to the fatherless and be able to transfer a rich spiritual inheritance to future generations. This is how the Kingdom advances without delay.

2. **Apostles are called to build the Kingdom and the church.**

"10...according to the grace of God which was given to me, as a wise master builder I have laid the foundation, and another builds on it. But let each one take heed how he builds on it."
1 Corinthians 3.10

We learned that a master builder is one who designs the plans of a building before it is built—God gave apostles the plan to build His Kingdom and church. This is a fundamental role for an apostle. A true Kingdom builder is not satisfied with having a large church. Therefore, a genuine apostle will not feel fully satisfied or a complete sense of accomplishment unless he is training and edifying people and things that are important for the Kingdom; this gives meaning to his life.

What does it mean to edify?

In Greek, the word for **edify** is *"oikodomeo"*; it refers to the act of building a house or structure; a spiritual promotion, growth, progress, and the development of character.

One role or responsibility of the apostle is to help believers mature and develop the character of Christ through patient laboring. The life and character of every individual cannot be built overnight; hence, the reason why it is not a job for just anybody. God gave apostles the virtue of patience which they need to build the lives of others without giving up, and the wisdom to know how to do it. The apostle is a master builder; an expert when it comes to building or creating something.

Believers are Buildings of God

"⁹For we are God's fellow workers; you are God's field, you are God's building." 1 Corinthians 3.9

Apostles know the design needed to build the structure of each believer; they know how to prepare and train them until they become a living stone in the Father's building.

"⁹...not returning evil for evil or reviling for reviling, but on the contrary blessing, knowing that you were called to this, that you may inherit a blessing." 1 Peter 2.5

What is the main reason for edifying believers?

The fundamental reason why Christians must be edified is to create a dwelling place for God. The main objective in the life of an apostle is to build a house in the hearts of the people where our Heavenly Father can live and have communion with his children—nothing causes greater joy in the heart of an apostle.

"²¹...in whom the whole building, being fitted together, grows into a holy temple in the Lord, ²²in whom you also are being built together for a dwelling place of God in the Spirit."
Ephesians 2.21, 22

Note that an apostle builds beyond the church or God's people; they also build the Kingdom, the church, and believers around the world. This is because the apostle has a strong passion and a powerful clear vision to build cities and establish and extend the Kingdom of God.

3. **Apostles establish the foundation of the apostolic doctrine in the church.**

"[20]...having been built on the foundation of the apostles and prophets, Jesus Christ Himself being the chief cornerstone..." Ephesians 2.20

Nowadays, ministries fall and disappear because apostles never laid a solid foundation on which to establish them. Apostles and prophets are called to establish the foundation of Christianity.

What is a doctrine?

A doctrine is a set of teachings that have to do with Jesus: who He is as the Son of God, His birth, purpose, crucifixion, death, and resurrection. Furthermore, it includes the basic teachings on the laying of hands, baptisms, faith, and more.

"[9]Whoever transgresses and does not abide in the doctrine of Christ does not have God. He who abides in the doctrine of Christ has both the Father and the Son." 2 John 1.9

One function of the apostle is to establish the foundation and apostolic doctrine in the local church. You might have noticed that in the New Testament, every church was founded by apostles. After they established the churches and confirmed that they were growing in sound doctrine, they delegated authority over a pastor who would continue the work. In the New Testament, we never see a pastor laying the foundation for a church because this is the function of the apostolic ministry.

4. Apostles plant and establish churches and ministries.

"6I (Paul) planted, Apollos watered..."
1 Corinthians 3.6 — Amplified Bible

Another responsibility of an apostle is to establish churches from ground zero; to open churches where there are none. When this is done, the apostle establishes the government, ordains elders and ministers, and selects a pastor to guide the church.

Some apostles might decide to stay and supervise the church and its growth; others will continue on their journey of establishing more churches. Sometimes, apostles adopt churches; they help lay the foundation of the doctrine and establish the proper structure of government so they can continue to grow according to the divine design.

5. Apostles establish the order and structure of authority and government in the churches.

Most ministries cannot fight the enemy because they failed to establish the proper governmental structure; due to the same, they lose the souls they won. Most churches do not have a set of guidelines for authority and government; hence, the reason many become casualties of spiritual warfare. Many Christian leaders, who are not subject to a structure of authority and who failed to obtain the support of an apostle, enter into spiritual warfare for the city but end up suffering the consequences together with their congregation.

"5For this reason I left you in Crete, that you should set in order the things that are lacking, and appoint elders in every city as I commanded you." Titus 1.5

One role of the apostle is to organize the leadership in the church: the ministers, elders, and to establish the five-fold ministries found in Ephesians 4.11. Furthermore, they should establish the proper order of authority: Jesus as the head and end with the believer. If apostles carry out this responsibility correctly, the church will grow, multiply, and take by force the territory seized by the enemy; without the fear of what the enemy might try to do to stop it. When the church functions in the perfect order established by God, neither Satan nor his cunning plans will work. The church that functions under the proper order and structure of leadership and government will always prevail over the works of its enemies.

What should be the structure of government in the local or global church?

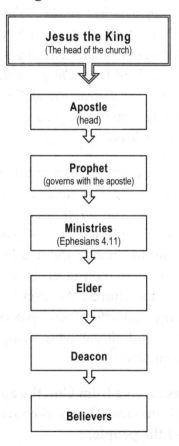

Every church operates differently in their level of authority, but it is the apostle who establishes that authority and structure of government in order to align the church to the divine design. For that reason, when a pastor wants to establish his own ministry, he should seek the advice of an apostle.

"³For I indeed, as absent in body but present in spirit, have already judged (as though I were present) him who has so done this deed. ⁴In the name of our Lord Jesus Christ, when you are gathered together, along with my spirit, with the power of our Lord Jesus Christ, ⁵deliver such a one to Satan for the destruction of the flesh, that his spirit may be saved in the day of the Lord Jesus." 1 Corinthians 5.3-5

Apostles also judge and establish judgment and discipline against sin in the church. This is part of the divine order that they are able to enforce by the grace that was given to them; it is one way to remove the anathema from the people and how the presence of God is able to remain in the church. As seen in the previous verse, the apostle Paul passed judgment against an individual who was practicing the sin of fornication.

6. **Apostles receive from God the ability to cause a transformation in the minds and hearts of the people.**

"²And do not be conformed to this world, but be transformed by the renewing of your mind, that you

may prove what is that good and acceptable and perfect will of God..." Romans 12.2

Apostles are responsible for transforming the minds of the Christian people by destroying old paradigms, legalistic points of view, and negative mentalities; also, by helping the people to grow and mature spiritually. These things are only made possible by the grace of God. Apostles experience the pain of persecution when they challenge and destroy old traditions and mentalities, but when welcomed by the people, they are able to impact and cause great changes in their lives.

7. **Apostles are called to equip and train believers for the work of the ministry.**

"12...for the equipping of the saints for the work of ministry, for the edifying of the body of Christ." Ephesians 4.12

The role of an apostle is to be a mentor; to train, equip, and prepare believers until they are able to work and serve effectively in the ministry. Also, they are to persevere until everyone is mature enough to carry out the calling of God in their lives. When this happens, the final revival will take place. Apostles also supervise and administrate the ministerial offices found in Ephesians 4.11. Apostles are able to accomplish this with the gift they have to identify the gifts in other believers. He takes a believer and places him in a place or sphere where his gifts are effective; he teaches and guides the believer in the process. When he is able to do it right, he stands back and supervises, allowing him the opportunity to grow, develop, and mature.

8. **Apostles are called to lead the war against the enemy and to take over the city.**

Apostles have a governmental authority with which they establish decrees in the spirit; they are capable of destroying principalities and strongholds in the city. They receive the design from God to take over the city and guide the leadership and the people to do it—Paul did it in Thessalonica and Ephesus.

9. **Apostles receive the mysteries of the Kingdom and reveal them to the church.**

"5[This mystery] was never disclosed to human beings in past generations as it has now been revealed to His holy apostles (consecrated messengers) and prophets by the [Holy] Spirit."
Ephesians 3.5—Amplified Bible

An apostle receives divine revelations from the Holy Spirit; these are truths found in the Word that have not been seen. The apostle receives the revelations and uses them to edify the believers; hence, the reason why the teaching or preaching from an apostle brings such a strong impartation and authority into the spirit of a believer that it changes him.

10. Apostles proclaim the Kingdom with manifestations of power, signs, and wonders.

"43Then fear came upon every soul, and many wonders and signs were done through the apostles." Acts 2.43

Each word from an apostle is delivered with the visible demonstration of the power of God which comes in the form of signs, miracles, healing, prophecy, and the gifts of the Holy Spirit, among many more. This was the ministry of Jesus: to teach, preach, heal the sick, and rebuke demons.

When we speak of the functions of an apostle, we are not referring to the signs and wonders of his ministry. The role or function of an apostle is not to perform miracles or to have the heart of a father. The main responsibility, role, or function of an apostle is to exercise his paternity over his spiritual children; to build the Kingdom and the church, to lay the foundation of the apostolic doctrine, to establish new churches, adopt ministries, and to create and organize the structure of government and authority in the church. The apostle should equip the people to serve in the ministry; he should cause a transformation in their hearts and minds, and lead the war against the enemy to take over the city.

The functions of an apostle are vitally important to the body of Christ and for the purpose of God with our generation. We need to understand this and welcome the apostles for what they are so they can function to their fullest ability. Otherwise, we will be unable to experience the flow of the new wine and a reformation in society and man-kind as a whole.

5

Different Types of Apostles and Their Sphere of Influence

Now we know what an apostle is and the Biblical signs and essential functions that determine who he is. In this chapter, we will learn about the different types of apostles and their sphere of influence. Many apostles are successful in certain countries, cities, or regions. However, when they try to do the same thing elsewhere, they fail. Why? Because God gives each apostle a sphere; a specific zone of influence within which he can exercise the power and authority God has given him and be successful at it. If the apostle leaves that circle, he will fail unless God sends him outside the sphere of influence in which he usually operates. If the apostle is led by God to leave his sphere of influence to do a job for a determined amount of time, God will stand by his side and show His support.

It was previously said that during the reign of Alexander the Great, the commander of the naval force was called an apostle; this man was sent to carry out a specific task under the authority of the king. He was sent to a specific place with the sole objective of enlarging the Kingdom for Alexander the Great. Jesus, as the King of the Kingdom of God, sends each of His apostles to specific places to carry out specific missions in order to establish His Kingdom. Apostles are commissioned by God and given a sphere of influence and a measure of grace according to their mission.

What is a sphere of influence?

A sphere of influence is the place or specific area where the influence of the apostle is most effective and where he is able to function to his fullest capacity. Paul established that he was an apostle within the limits of his sphere of influence. In other words, an apostle cannot exercise his authority in a place or area where God has not commissioned him to be.

"13But we will not boast of things without our measure, but according to the measure of the rule which God hath distributed to us, a measure to reach even unto you."
2 Corinthians 10.13

In Greek, the word for **rule** is *"kanon"*; it means a measuring rod or rule; a carpenter's line or measuring tape; a definitely bounded or fixed space within the limits of which one's power of influence is confined; the province assigned; an apostle's sphere of activity or place where he is able to exercise his authority.

God gave us a *"kanon"*; a measuring rod that helps us operate within our area of influence—it does not allow us to leave the area where He placed us, and it keeps us in line. Every believer has a *"kanon"* or area of influence in which he can establish and extend the Kingdom effectively.

What is the measure of grace?

"13...but according to the measure of the rule which God hath distributed to us..." 2 Corinthians 10.13

The Greek word for **measure** is *"metron"*; it means an instrument for measuring. When the Bible mentions the word **measure**, it refers to a measure of anointing—this is the same word used to speak of the measure of anointing of Jesus.

"34For He whom God has sent speaks the words of God, for God does not give the Spirit by measure." John 3.34

Jesus was the only man who had the anointing of the Holy Spirit without measure. Everyone has a measure of faith because together, we are the body of Christ in whom the fullness of grace resides.

The measure of grace is given according to:

❖ **The gift given by God.**

> *"7But to each one of us grace was given according to the measure of Christ's gift."* Ephesians 4.7

The measure of grace, anointing, and authority that are in a man or a woman depend on the gift God gave them. This is true because some apostles are called and gifted by the Lord to touch multitudes while others receive the gift or calling that is limited to the local level; these do not need a mantle of grace as great or as large as the apostle that is called to touch the nations around the world.

❖ **The will of God.**

"11But one and the same Spirit works all these things, distributing to each one individually as He wills." 1 Corinthians 12.11

We cannot choose the level of grace and anointing we are to receive; it is up to God. He decides which gift and how much grace to give us according to His perfect will.

Some apostles, prophets, evangelists, pastors, and teachers have a measure of grace that is greater than others; that measure should be recognized and respected. Who decided it should be like this? God! Therefore, we must submit to His perfect will and follow His plan without standing in the way of what He is doing.

In the New Testament, 22 apostles are mentioned; they can be identified by name and by what they did. Jacob, the brother of Jesus, stood out among the rest. He was not one of the twelve, but he did become the leader of the apostles in Jerusalem. There was a measure of grace upon his life that was greater than the rest.

"¹³And after they had become silent, James answered, saying, "Men and brethren, listen to me: ¹⁹Therefore I judge that we should not trouble those from among the Gentiles who are turning to God." Acts 15.13, 19

Peter was given the grace to be among the Jews while Paul was given the grace for the gentiles. Each had his own sphere of influence and a measure of grace which were recognized and respected by their peers; that is why they were successful and produced abundant fruit for the Kingdom. It is important for us to recognize the apostles that have a greater measure of grace so we can respect and honor them according to that measure.

Some apostles are called only to influence the culture or the Hispanic population, but when they try to cross over that limit to influence others, they lose their effectiveness and fail. Some afro-American apostles received the grace to reach only the people of their own race—that is their area of influence and if they try to reach other cultures, they will fail. However, God gave some apos-tles a multi-cultural grace. In other words, the grace to influence a variety of people: Hispanics, Caucasians, Afro-Americans, and others.

You cannot be an apostle over an area that was not given to you by God or over people who reject you. In my experience as an apostle, God gave me a measure of grace with the Hispanic population first, but He also gave me the grace to influence the Caucasians and the Afro-American population. I consider myself a multi-cultural apostle.

What different types of apostles exist in the body of Christ?

1. The pioneer

An apostle that is a pioneer is one that establishes churches in new territories. Furthermore, he lays the foundation, establishes the Christian doctrine, identifies the leadership, edifies the five-fold ministries found in Ephesians 4.11, and selects the headship or pastor; when the church is strong and in order, this apostle goes to another place to continue his pioneer work.

Apostles who are pioneers pave the way for others; they are first to establish churches for the Kingdom in places where there were none. They start the work from ground zero and turn it into a powerful influential church. In the first stages, they operate in all the ministries found in Ephesians 4.11; they evangelize, teach, prophesy, and minister the people as pastors. The prophet, evangelist, pastor, and teacher need the apostle's help. However, the apostle has the ability to carry out all the functions needed to establish a church because he is capable of operating in the four ministries. They quickly identify the people who are gifted to carry out the Ephesians 4.11 ministries and train them to help him carry the mission forward. This type of apostle always establishes strong churches because of the measure of his gift—which few people have. Paul is an example of a pioneer apostle; Apollos was not.

2. **The apostle of the city**

"⁸...and you shall be witnesses to Me in Jerusalem..." Acts 1.8

This apostle is sent by God to build a church for the city and establish himself there. This type of apostle is also called the apostle of Jerusalem.

What is a church for the city?

This type of church is a regional apostolic center that provides the spiritual covering, paternity, service, and resources to other churches in the city.

Why does God send an apostle to build a church for the city?

❖ To extend the Kingdom of God by force. In other words, the purpose of a city church is to impact society and change the spiritual atmosphere of that place.

"1Therefore I exhort first of all that supplications, prayers, intercessions, and giving of thanks be made for all men, 2for kings and all who are in authority, that we may lead a quiet and peaceable life in all godliness and reverence." 1 Timothy 2.1, 2

❖ To gather the harvest. The apostle sees the multitude and feels great passion to win the lost for Christ.

"41Then those who gladly received his word were baptized; and that day about three thousand souls were added to them." Acts 2.41

❖ To develop churches until they become regional apostolic centers at the city level.

The apostle of the city provides the resources, tools, training, and weaponry needed to destroy the enemy's strongholds; he is also responsible for identifying the Ephesians 4.11 ministries. Furthermore, he must stay in the city most of the time to build the regional apostolic center. The ministry of the apostle focuses mainly on building a church for the city.

3. **The apostle sent to the nation, neighboring countries, or to a certain ethnic group.**

"8...and you shall be witnesses to Me in Jerusalem, and in all Judea and Samaria..." Acts 1.8

This apostle is called to serve in Judea and Samaria. In other words, this apostle serves the area around the regional center. For instance, the Hispanic church in the United States that also serves Mexico, Central America, and South America.

The mission of this apostle is to visit churches that are already strong apostolic centers in the city and offer resources, training, and tools; he will offer to teach them how to take over the city and help them become stronger and with greater influence in the area. This type of apostle unites the local churches to teach and minister to them; he helps them to grow and mature until they become great and powerful.

As for me, I travel to countries where there is an apostle with whom I have a relation-ship with; someone who is significant or fundamental for what God wants to do in the nation. Also, I make sure that I am able to teach in seminars and conferences in which I can train the local pastors. Also, I bring together the government officials and minister to them. Before leaving, I end my visit with an evangelistic and miracle crusade in a stadium—this is done to raise a harvest of souls. These things touch the hearts of the pastors, the government officials, the church, and the people, in such a way, that the entire country is strengthened. My calling is to be an apostle for the city but also for the nations.

4. **The apostle to the world.**

"8... and to the end of the earth." Acts 1.8

This apostle is commissioned by God to go to the end of the earth. He adapts to the ethnic culture wherever he goes and is able to overcome any barriers of traditions, culture, or language. For example, the Apostle Paul.

It is hard for this type of apostle to delay his leaving a city for long because of his itinerary and calling to the nations of the earth. The calling of this type of apostle is not to establish churches but to edify the body of Christ around the world; to accomplish this, he must travel constantly.

Testimony: something very interesting happened to me after I was commissioned to be an apostle. I was traveling extensively which caused me to be absent too many Sunday's from my own church. I noticed the growth of the local church had stopped. I couldn't explain what was happening since God had told me that the church would continue to grow even though I was traveling. I felt I needed to eliminate most of my travel plans and stay at home, but this made me feel frustrated—the growth rate of the church remained the same though I was home.

What was the problem?

The problem was in the balance of things; it had nothing to do with traveling too much or not. God spoke to me and led me to find a balance between being at home and traveling the nations. When I spent too much time traveling, the church suffered. When I spent too much time at home, the mantle of anointing would diminish. The solution to my dilemma was found in knowing how to balance my busy agenda. Now, when I travel, I am away from home on weekdays; I am back in church for the Sunday services. This is a good balance because the mantle expands, the church continues to grow, and my calling to the nations is carried out. God blesses us when we balance our agenda. Amen!

5. The apostle that is a high ranking warrior.

This apostle has the grace of God to conquer a territory and train believers and the leadership to fight the war. This type of apostle is not the leader of a particular church or group of churches. In actuality, he leads the church as a whole into spiritual warfare. God anoints many of these apostles to serve in specific areas including: deliverance, finances, intercession, and spiritual warfare. They have a special anointing to minister in one or two areas in particular.

6. The apostle of a local church

This type of apostle joins forces with the apostle of the city. He helps to create strategies and is called to identify, detect, develop, and train people in the five-fold ministries. He also helps the general apostle of the church to establish the Christian doctrine and to lead the rest of the leadership.

In conclusion, let us remember that no one starts as an apostle. Most apostles start out as evangelists, pastors, teachers, or prophets. Finally, God commissions them as apostles to carry out a specific mission.

Are you an apostle? What type of an apostle are you? Are you a pioneer? Are you called to build a city? Are you called to the city and the neighboring nations? Are you an apostle sent to the ends of the earth? Are you a warrior called to train the people for warfare? Are you called to work in a local church? What is your sphere of influence? What is your measure of grace? Are you called to influence a particular type of people, nation, or race?

Through all of this, we must not lose sight of the fact that Jesus is the only one who calls people to the apostolic ministry. Jesus is the one who commissions apostles to go to a specific place and gives the authority needed to operate in that place. If we follow this rule and measure, we will receive the grace and anointing from God to successfully do our job. Today, countless men call themselves apostles, but they do not have the character or ministerial results that determine their status. Other apostles are operating outside of their area of influence and that is why they fail. The most important thing to remember is not the gift but the will of God. To be effective, the apostle must be in the perfect will of God for his life and calling.

6

Tools Used by the Apostle to Build

We know the apostle is a wise teacher and master builder of the Kingdom; he has the grace given by God to see something in the spirit and carry it out in the natural.

The apostle receives the design to build his church because he is a builder of people, because he is passionate about seeing God's building erected, and because it is in him to help every believer become a living stone in that building. This chapter will teach us what it means to build in the spirit and what tools are needed to do the job.

What does it mean to build in the spirit?

To build in the spirit is the ability to penetrate the spirit realm in a specific area and destroy the power of darkness, strongholds, mental paradigms, and establish an open heaven over that area in order to help believers mature spiritually. Therefore, to build in the spirit is far more than just simple teaching or leading worship services; it is more than trying to inspire the people. To build, the apostle must practice spiritual warfare and establish an open heaven over a territory.

How does an apostle build in the spirit?

"10...the grace of God which was given to me, as a wise master builder..." 1 Corinthians 3.10

The apostle builds according to the Biblical design or pattern for a specific moment. This method enables him to build something that will touch future generations, that will help gather and save the harvest, and above all, that will cause the glory of God to descend.

God's Pattern or Design

There is nothing more frustrating in life than not knowing the design or how something works. In our experience, not knowing the purpose or reason why God gives us a plan or design is the greatest frustration we can suffer. God, the creator of mankind, has the perfect design for our lives that will help us have a happy family and show us how to be good parents and children. Also, He has a special design for our spiritual growth, ministry, and church; this is, so the spiritual family can also prosper and rejoice. Everything in heaven and on earth was created by God after giving it purpose.

God Has the Original Pattern or Design

God is so creative that the seven billion people living on this earth have different DNA's. This means that everybody is an original design; hence, the reason why something that works for one person does not work for the other. Therefore, we do not need to try to imitate other people; all we need to do is ask God for the original design for our lives which is unique and cannot be duplicated.

The only requirement needed for God to place His glory over an individual, ministry, or nation is for there to be a divine order and for these to be built according His design.

What is a pattern or design?

"¹⁰Son of man, describe the temple to the house of Israel, that they may be ashamed of their iniquities; and let them measure the pattern. ¹¹And if they are ashamed of all that they have done, make known to them the design of the temple and its arrangement, its exits and its entrances, its entire design and all its ordinances, all its forms and all its laws. Write it down in their sight, so that they may keep its whole design and all its ordinances, and perform them." Ezekiel 43.10, 11

The pattern or design is the detailed plan of action that God gives a man or a woman. This plan includes: the nature of the plan, exits, entryways, shape, description, configurations, rules, and laws that must be implemented for His Kingdom. A design is a vision given in full detail.

To whom does God give the pattern or design of His work?

God gives the design of his vision to a man or woman He commissions as an apostle and who is sent to carry it out with authority and ability. Moses was such a man.

"8And let them make Me a sanctuary, that I may dwell among them. 9According to all that I show you, that is, the pattern of the tabernacle and the pattern of all its furnishings, just so you shall make it." Exodus 25.8, 9

When something is built without God's design, it will fail God's test of fire; it will burn without reaping a reward because it is considered the works of the flesh: wood, hay, or stubble. However, if it is done according to God's design, it will bear abundant fruit, pass the test of fire, and be purified and perfected like gold, silver, and precious stones. Today, God is sharing His designs with His apostles—Kingdom builders—to build His church; one that is strong enough to withstand every test and be triumphant and sanctified as it extends the Kingdom to the ends of the earth.

How do apostles receive God's pattern or design?

"12Then the LORD said to Moses, "Come up to Me on the mountain and be there; and I will give you tablets of

stone, and the law and commandments which I have written, that you may teach them." Exodus 24.12

Moses received the design on the mountain; he was fasting, praying, and alone with God. This is the same way apostles receive the design today. As previously explained, the calling of God to His apostles is a revelation given in private, from Jesus to the spirit of man. This calling is later confirmed by men of great spiritual standing who publicly declare God's will for that man.

What are the consequences of not building according to God's pattern or design?

"⁶When they came to the threshing floor of Nacon, Uzzah reached out and took hold of the ark of God, because the oxen stumbled. ⁷The LORD's anger burned against Uzzah because of his irreverent act; therefore God struck him down and he died there beside the ark of God." 2 Samuel 6.6, 7—NIV

When the glory of God descends, it could cause blessing or judgment. If we do things according to God's divine order and design, His glory will bring blessings. However, if we do things out of order and not according to His design, it will cause judgment.

In the verse you just read, it says that Uzzah was struck down because of his irreverent act; he had mistakenly become familiarized with the glory of God.

What was the divine design in this case?

God had given strict instructions to Moses concerning the Ark. He had established that it should only be carried on the shoulders of Levites—no one was allowed to touch it or to look at its contents. David wanted to take the Ark back to the city of David but did not follow God's specific instructions for moving it. He put men like Uzzah and his brother, who were not Levites, to transport the Ark on a new cart pulled by oxen. This is symbolic of the fact that the glory of God cannot be touched—it cannot be seen in the flesh but in the spirit.

God's judgment came upon Uzzah because he did not follow God's design. Why was Uzzah punished and not David? Because David's heart was pure; his motives were right. Uzzah, on the other hand, became familiarized with the Ark during its stay in his father's house. The Ark was in Abinadab's house for quite some time and by looking at it every day, Uzzah lost his respect and reverence for it; hence, the reason why he touched it with irreverence not fearing God's judgment. This should teach us never to adopt such an attitude towards the presence of God or His glory.

How did Jesus receive the pattern or design for His church?

Before Jesus, there was no church. We were all separated from God due to our sins; we did not have access to His presence. Jesus dedicated His life to seeking the Father's perfect will and carrying it out on earth. He received the design for the church during His prayer time. There, the Father showed him that He had to choose disciples and teach them to heal, rebuke demons, preach, and later, reveal the Father to them. These would eventually lead the way to Jesus commissioning them to be apostles and to expand His Kingdom to the ends of the earth by establishing churches and training other disciples to do the same for future generations. This is how the generation of His time and future generations would receive the benefits of the sacrifice of the cross and the teachings shared with His disciples during the three years He spent with them.

"13And He went up on the mountain and called to Him those He Himself wanted. And they came to Him. 14Then He appointed twelve, that they might be with Him and that He might send them out to preach, 15and to have power to heal sicknesses and to cast out demons." Mark 3.13-15

If we want to do God's will and receive the design of what we need to do, we must go to the *mountain*—our secret place—and spend time alone with God while fasting and praying. We must go to the mountain and ask God in prayer to reveal His design to us.

The Original Pattern or Design of the Five-fold Ministries

In Genesis 1.28, we notice that from the moment that God created man, he deviates from his original design. God commissions him to go and multiply and fill the land; to subdue and be lord over all creation. Instead of obeying, man did the one thing God had asked him not to do. Later, in Genesis 11.1-4, we learn that all the people spoke only one language; they had settled in one area, and once again, they chose to deviate from God's design. They made the mistake of trying to make a name for themselves by building the Tower of Babel. The construction of this tower was one more way to demonstrate the tendency of man to disobey and his sense of independence from God; it was also an action that tried to substitute the original and the authentic with man's designs, instead of following the divine plan.

"¹Now the whole earth had one language and one speech. ²And it came to pass, as they journeyed from the east, that they found a plain in the land of Shinar, and they dwelt there. ³Then they said to one another, "Come, let us make bricks and bake them thoroughly." They had brick for stone, and they had asphalt for

mortar. *4And they said, "Come, let us build ourselves a city, and a tower whose top is in the heavens; let us make a name for ourselves, lest we be scattered abroad over the face of the whole earth." Genesis 11.1-4*

There is an original design given by God to the church that would help every believer reach the measure of the stature of the perfect man. This design is the five-fold ministries: apostle, prophet, evangelist, pastor, and teacher. Traditionally speaking, the work of the ministry was considered to be a job for the pastor; he would be the only one to take care of the church's needs. However, this goes against God's design. Through the following illustration, you will be able to see clearly how God's original design works in the church:

"11And He Himself gave some to be apostles, some prophets, some evangelists, and some pastors and teachers." Ephesians 4.11

Why did God restore the five-fold ministries?

The Lord, in His infinite wisdom and knowledge of the times, restored the five-fold ministries with the purpose of perfecting the believers—it is crucial for us to be ready for the spiritual reformation that will shake our nations.

"12...for the equipping of the saints for the work of ministry..." Ephesians 4.12

The Greek word for **equipping** is *"katartismos"*; it means to prepare and train the saints—*believers*. To enhance the definition of this world we can say it is the total and complete preparation of a believer in every area: to teach, train, activate, indoctrinate, give him tools, and teach him how to use them. These things are applicable in the following areas: personal, family life, ministry, character, and more.

The ministry of the pastor, evangelist, and teacher were restored throughout the previous century. These days, God is restoring the ministry of the apostle because they are called to carry out the last part of this verse: *"...for the equipping of the saints."*

The apostle is the master builder who will build the Kingdom of God in every corner of the earth.

What tools are used by the apostle to build the Kingdom?

God gives the apostle the design or Biblical pattern for His church and the tools and resources he will need to build it; these tools are:

1. The apostolic authority

"⁸For even if I should boast somewhat more about our authority, which the Lord gave us for edification and not for your destruction, I shall not be ashamed." 2 Corinthians 10.8

The apostolic authority is a powerful tool with which the apostle can build or discipline the people. It is also useful when he passes judgment against the works and plans that the enemy tries to execute to try and stop the building of the church of Christ.

2. The apostolic fatherhood

The apostle builds a church or ministry like a family—with a father and several children. He teaches them to love and honor their heavenly Father; he raises and trains them until they reach spiritual maturity. The apostle is a father who has great passion to reproduce his DNA in others and lead them to discover their purpose in God. This process is essential because in order to build a ministry or church he has to be more than a supervisor or leader— he must be a father.

3. The knowledge of God's ways

An apostle is not someone who appears or is created over night; he is a man whose heart was formed in the desert and who has experienced intense pressure and calamity. It is during this process that he gets to know God and His ways; hence, the reason he is able to edify others through his experiences with God.

"7He made known His ways to Moses, His acts to the children of Israel." Psalms 103.7

To discover God's ways, we must experience His presence; we must receive the revelation of who He is and be mature enough to understand Him. We must learn His methods, why He does what He does, when He makes a move, and why. In other words, we must know the how, when, and why of God. This is the reason why only an apostle, who has learned great lessons through his experiences with God, is able to build the church according to God's divine designs.

4. The communion with the Holy Spirit

"14The grace of the Lord Jesus Christ, and the love of God, and the communion of the Holy Spirit be with you all. Amen." 2 Corinthians 13.14

The Greek word for **communion** is *"koinonia"*; it has two definitions:

❖ Having the same life in common.

❖ Having the same passion and purpose in common.

The heart of the apostle is continually attached to the same eternal life of the Holy Spirit; it also has the same passion to build the Kingdom of God.

The eternal life of the Holy Spirit is to build and extend the Kingdom of God. The apostle that has a life in unity with the Holy Spirit wants to build the Kingdom and has the ability to do it. In that communion, the apostle is able to hear the voice of God with clarity and receives the guidelines to build His church.

5. Divine wisdom

The seal of an architect that operates in the spirit is divine wisdom; this is one of the most important characteristics of the apostolic ministry.

"3Through skillful and godly Wisdom is a house (a life, a home, a family) built, and by understanding it is established [on a sound and good foundation]." Proverbs 24.3 — Amplified Bible

El Rey Jesus church is the perfect example of a house of God that was built based on a divine plan, with divine wisdom, and according to the plans God provided.

An apostle needs certain administrative skills to organize and the ability of a master builder to lay the foundation. However, these are not enough; he needs divine wisdom to complete the project according to God's specifications. In other words, the apostle not only builds organizations with the natural tools of methodology, but he also builds men and churches with divine wisdom.

What is wisdom?

Wisdom is a virtue in God's character which consists in knowing the true nature of things— visible and invisible—and knowing how to deal with them correctly and at the right time.

"[6]However, we speak wisdom among those who are mature, yet not the wisdom of this age, nor of the rulers of this age, who are coming to nothing."
1 Corinthians 2.6

Natural characteristics of divine wisdom:

❖ Wisdom is the highest level of spiritual maturity we can hope to reach; that is why we must want it and value it as something to be treasured.

"⁵If any of you lacks wisdom, let him ask of God, who gives to all liberally and without reproach, and it will be given to him." James 1.5

❖ Divine wisdom comes from the mind of God and works together with two other virtues found in the Deity: fear of the Lord and His sovereignty.

❖ Wisdom never works independently of the presence of God because it relates to the purpose, designs, determinations, and dealings of God.

❖ Wisdom has nothing to do with the natural age of an individual since most people reach old age having never known it.

❖ God's wisdom is a group of practical principles that can be applied to our daily living; Salomon called them proverbs.

What is a proverb?

A proverb is a short saying that is full of God's wisdom; it is a norm, rule, deep thought, method, law, or divine guide for daily living.

For instance:

- "No one can be completely accepted until he is completely rejected."

- "It is better to be criticized for taking action than to be ignored for doing nothing."

- "You will enjoy a significant level of success in that which is an obsession for you."

- "God does not consider your past when determining your future."

- "Everything that has life grows and prospers."

- "The meaning of life is not found in the similarity with others but in your differences."

- "The worth of your friendships is measured by their contributions into your needs."

How can we understand the nature of wisdom?

Although it might seem redundant, to understand the nature of wisdom one must acquire understanding.

What is the meaning of understanding?

Understanding means to know the original purpose of why something was created, the principles with which it operates, and its function.

If you do not know who you are in God, you are not lord over your own life. That is why people who are unsure of their identity are inclined to imitate the identity or personality of others. To do God's will in your life, you must know who you are and understand why you were created.

"*12He who is devoid of wisdom despises his neighbor, but a man of understanding holds his peace.*" Proverbs 11.12

Divine wisdom is the ability to understand the "why" of all things in order to know what to do, when to do it, and how to get it done. Wisdom means to have an understanding of what is happening in order to know how to deal with a situation the right way and at the right time. The word *wise* means according to science, understanding, and knowledge.

"*7Husbands, likewise, dwell with them with **understanding**, giving honor to the wife, as to the weaker vessel, and as being heirs together of the* *grace of life, that your prayers may not be hindered." 1 Peter 3.7*

It is very hard for a man to live with his wife if he does not know her. He must learn to understand how her spirit, body, and soul work in order to keep the unity and joy in the marriage relationship and to avoid having anything disrupt his relationship with God.

6. The revelation of the Word and the mysteries of God

God gave the apostle unlimited access to his mysteries with which he can activate, impart, demonstrate, and transform people. These revelations are powerful tools found in Scripture, that for some unknown reason, we had not seen before. However, when the apostle receives them, he uses them to edify the people. It is a common occurrence for an apostle to receive new revelations of the Word. For the most part, the apostle does not repeat his messages because God continuously gives him the first fruit of his revelation. In this way, he is able to edify the people with the present truth—his messages are not recycled. This does not imply that the truths we have heard and learned are invalid. On the contrary, we must appreciate them and teach them to others. Furthermore, the revelations the apostle receives are fundamental and supported by Scripture which means that they are all found in the Word.

7. The fear of the Lord

"31Then the churches throughout all Judea, Galilee, and Samaria had peace and were edified. And walking in the fear of the Lord and in the comfort of the Holy Spirit, they were multiplied." Acts 9.31

The fear of the Lord is the respect and reverence we have towards Him; it has nothing to do with a fear or phobia. To have the fear of the Lord means to be passionate about pleasing Him and to greatly fear the possibility of displeasing Him. The apostle builds with great fear of the Lord because he is passionate to please Him and do His perfect will.

8. The apostle builds with the gift of leadership and administration

The apostle has the ability to unite people with the leadership and to put them to work in the right place. Also, he has the skill to plan short-term and long-term strategies. Furthermore, because he is a good administrator, the apostle knows how to use the resources available to him wisely and effectively.

9. The apostle builds with his personal experiences

In the process of growing and maturing, we are likely to make many mistakes. The apostle learns from his personal mistakes and experiences and uses that knowledge to build others. He learns what to do and what not to do precisely because of the diverse situations and challenges he endures and overcomes.

10. The apostle builds with love.

"¹...now concerning things offered to idols: We know that we all have knowledge. Knowledge puffs up, but love edifies." 1 Corinthians 8.1

Love is the most notable virtue in the life and character of an apostle. The force behind the power to build is the great love he has for God and the people.

We know that building in the spirit means to destroy the enemy's spiritual strongholds in a specific area—to break mental strongholds and establish an open heaven in order to help the people grow spiritually. We also know that the apostle builds according to God's design and pattern for today. He receives instruction from the Holy Spirit concerning the precise moment and place where he should challenge and fight the enemy, destroy all strongholds, and establish His Kingdom.

To build according to Biblical design causes the manifestation of the glory of God, and not doing it causes judgment. God provided the right master builders to do the job: the apostle, prophet, pastor, teacher, and evangelist. Also, the main builder on earth, he who supervises the construction—the apostle—has all the tools he needs to carry out his task. He has authority, the heart of a father, an understanding of God's ways, a personal relationship with the Holy Spirit, divine wisdom, revelation of the Word, and fear of the Lord.

7

The Apostolic Mentality

Today, there are many erroneous ideas, mental strongholds, arguments, imaginations, and negative patterns of thought that are greatly affecting the body of Christ. That is why it is important to understand the apostolic mentality, renew our minds, and learn to identify true apostles—many paradigms, lies, and misunderstandings are stopping or preventing the move of God for this day.

What is a paradigm?

A paradigm is a negative, limited, and rigid mental structure because it originates from thoughts. This structure is rigid because it resists change and oppresses our level of hope; thus, reducing our vision of the future and our ability to see and perceive what is coming.

"5[Inasmuch as we] refute arguments and theories and reasonings and every proud and lofty thing that sets itself up against the [true] knowledge of God; and we lead every thought and purpose away captive into the obedience of Christ (the Messiah, the Anointed One)."
2 Corinthians 10.5—Amplified Bible

An example of a negative mental paradigm is the attitude to settle for less; this paradigm is influencing the church today. Pastors, leaders, and the people have accepted their present situation because they do not believe that something better can be done for the church, the Kingdom, or their generation.

The Holy Spirit wants to do something in our churches, but when He demonstrates something that is out of the ordinary and that we are not used to seeing, we resist it. God wants to give us new patterns and ways to lead our worship, discipleship groups, evangelistic ministry, and every other area, but we resist the change because of the countless mental paradigms we deal with on a daily basis. We have lost the vision for the future and have resigned ourselves to settle for less; this has caused the move of God to slow down or in some cases stop all together.

What are we going to do about it?

❖ **Present our bodies as a living sacrifice**

"1...I beseech you therefore, brethren, by the mercies of God, that you present your bodies a living sacrifice, holy, acceptable to God, which is your reasonable service." Romans 12.1

The words in this verse mean that we should allow God to do His perfect will through our bodies; this transforms us into a pleasing and living sacrifice before His presence. The body should not resist the leading of the Holy Spirit, and it should allow His perfect will to be done—that is our reasonable service.

❖ Renew our minds

"2And do not be conformed to this world, but be transformed by the renewing of your mind, that you may prove what is that good and acceptable and perfect will of God." Romans 12.2

The two key words in this verse are: conformed and transformed.

Conformed: to form, shape, block, adjust, adapt, or to resign oneself. The world and the religious system have formed and shaped us; they have influenced us to adapt a negative mentality, to think in terms of less than, and to be selfish. We must stop their influence and allow only the revelation of the Word to transform us, and destroy the old paradigms that prevent the move of God in our lives. We are called to be according to the image and likeness of the Son of God—not to resemble the old religious traditions which are worthless.

We must keep our hearts and minds open to the new things of the Spirit and to the changes he wants to bring to our lives; these things prepares us to welcome the new move of God.

"29For whom He foreknew, He also predestined to be conformed to the image of His Son, that He might be the firstborn among many brethren."
Romans 8.29

Transform: in Greek, *transform* is the word *"metamorphoo"*; it literally means to have an irreversible change. For instance, before a larva becomes a butterfly, it must endure a long process. After it becomes a butterfly, it never becomes a larva again because its change is irreversible. We need irreversible changes to take place in the mental structure of our church, and we need them now.

A mental transformation takes place when we renew our minds and patterns of thought; this is part of the process that will help us to be transformed into the image of Christ—this is how we will know the perfect will of God for our lives.

When the mind is not renewed, a transformation cannot be permanent.

For instance: people who smoke know that cigarette smoking is bad for their health; that is why they are always trying to quit. However, during this process, they might fail because their bodies are dominated or governed by their thoughts. Although they have all the information available on the dangers of smoking, their minds are still in need of a transformation that will lead them to make a radical change.

If these mental strongholds and paradigms are not destroyed, we will always be slaves to that habit, and sooner or later, we will go back to it—even if God has already delivered us in that area. We need to make irreversible changes in our minds before we can see the powerful move of God.

For years, the church has held on to a pastoral mentality not realizing that the Bible only mentions the role of the pastor 18 times but it mentions the apostle, his role, and respon-sibilities over 200 times. The church was estab-lished under an apostolic mentality not a pastoral mentality. Moreover, in the New Testament, we do not read about pastors planting new churches; we only read that apostles carried out their responsibilities. Today, the pastoral mentality is predominant in the church. This does not imply that the pastoral ministry is less important, of course it is important, but we must adapt the right mentality and give priority to the apostolic mentality.

Today, a shift is taking place; a transition from the pastoral mentality to the apostolic mentality. Do not misunderstand me. This does not mean that everyone is called to be an apostle or that we should stop being pastors— only Jesus can decide who is to become an apostle and what his mission and area of influence will be. However, to be a witness of the move of God, it is important for us to change our mentality and give priority to the apostolic way of thinking.

The Mentality of an Apostle vs. the Mentality of a Pastor

I want to make this clear: if God calls someone to be a pastor then that is what he should be. To be a pastor is a good thing. As a matter of fact, the office of a pastor is included in the five-fold ministries in Ephesians 4.11 which means that its role is very important in the edification of the body of Christ. The error is not in being a pastor but in maintaining a small mentality. You can be a pastor, evangelist, or teacher with an apostolic mentality to grow.

Pastoral Mentality	Apostolic Mentality
The pastor focuses mainly on the local church; he knows his congregation by name, birthdays, and phone number.	The apostle always has the Kingdom in mind; that is why his main focus is the church at a global level.
The pastor is focused on solving immediate situations; he loves his flock and is always taking care of their needs.	The apostle is focused on building something that lasts; his goal is to train men to pass the vision to future generations.
The pastor's mentality is at the local church level; his desire is to feed, take care, and be a shepherd to his flock.	The apostle focuses on the Kingdom and on the church as the body of Christ; he has a public and effective ministry and loves to minister to the people.
The pastor accepts the present situation without creating new strategies for the future; hence, the reason why he feels the need to belong to something greater in order to rise to higher levels.	The apostle wants an extreme change for the present situation. He always wants to rise to higher levels and to be on the cutting edge of what God is doing today.
The pastoral mentality does not know how to develop or make leaders; that is why they can only reach a certain level in their spiritual growth. When they are unable to grow any further, they get frustrated and leave. Sometimes, this is caused by the lack of identity in the pastor. As a result, the spiritual growth of his leaders represents a threat to him especially if they are women.	The apostolic mentality is to train and equip his spiritual children; leaders that serve and carry out the work of the ministry. The apostle delegates a job and concentrates on creating strategies for the kingdom. His ministry attracts or draws talented leaders to his side because he is able to identify and train them.
The pastor thinks about how to touch his generation; his teachings are mainly practical life-lessons useful for the present time.	The apostolic mentality focuses on how to influence the thousands; the apostle builds with future generations in mind.
The pastor inspires, encourages, and comforts the church with the "milk" of the Word; he helps his flock solve their immediate needs.	The apostle builds with the "meat" of the Word; he helps the people grow spiritually and become living stones in God's building.

Pastoral Mentality	Apostolic Mentality
The pastor avoids making his flock uncomfortable; thus, the reason why he resists change. This makes him a little inflexible to the will of God.	The apostle is flexible to the changes the Holy Spirit wants to make; that is why the apostolic church is on the cutting edge of the move of God.
The pastoral mentality has the ability to influence a few people.	The apostolic mentality has the ability to motivate, influence, and organize at a larger scale.
The pastor does not like to get involved in warfare; his mentality is not focused on war because his pastoral heart causes him to be passive.	The apostle is a fighter by nature; he fights the devil and his demons and leads the conquering of cities to extend the Kingdom.
The pastor does not like to take significant risks or risk his present sense of security. That is why, without the help of a ministry that has a larger vision, his church will always be small.	The apostle takes great steps of faith to extend the Kingdom of God; he is full of faith, audacious, an adventurer, and bold in the spirit.
The pastor establishes himself in one place and stays; he does not look to expand or open new territories and his tendency is not to take the first step in doing new things.	The apostle is a pioneer; he leads the exploration of new revelations, strategies, territories, and methods. His mentality is always to take the first step to establish the Kingdom.
The pastor has a "normal" way of thinking; it lines up with the society and culture around him.	The way an apostle thinks deviates from the norm; he is an uncommon man and a visionary.
The pastor's work habits are rather isolated. Many pastors do not have a spiritual covering—someone to whom they are accountable or who will take the time to minister to his needs.	The apostolic mentality includes submission as a life-style choice. The apostle is accountable to a spiritual authority that is above him and whom he respects, obeys, and honors.

How does the way our leader thinks affect us?

A leader's mentality will be the same as the people that serve under him. The same happens with the anointing; the same anointing that is over the leader will be over the people. Moreover, if the leader has a pastoral mentality, his congregation will be his flock but not his children; they will not have great dreams and stay at the same first level of care—they will never dream greater things than those they are already familiar with. They will take care of their church and of that which God has given them; they will be cautious and never risk anything at the possibility of exploring new territories or methods. They will not get involved in the war or in the conquest.

These believers are satisfied with touching their generation and supplying the basic needs of the believers. However, a leader with an apostolic mentality is always searching for new strategies to extend the Kingdom of God according to his sphere of influence. He will train spiritual leaders and establish them through a father-son relationship and later commission them to do the same. He will transmit his vision, the one God gave him, and together, they will develop the strategies received in the Spirit. The apostolic leader will raise a generation that will impact every realm and level of society; he will take risks and fight the opposition with determination and audacity as he builds the Kingdom of God around the world.

The purpose in making the difference between the pastoral and apostolic mentality is to demonstrate the importance and need of the apostolic ministry in the church and in the other ministries as well. As said before, the pastoral mentality is good, but it must grow into an apostolic mentality because we are in times of war, and we need to enter the powerful move of God which knocks at our door. God is using an apostle to lead this movement and to work together with the rest of the ministries. This is not about one man, but a team willing to do God's perfect will—God's way—and to stand firm and steady before the enemy so we can establish the Kingdom on earth. A pastor can ask: if I am a pastor, what shall I do? For your pastoral ministry to rise to a higher level, you must begin to associate with an apostle. The same thing applies to the other ministries found in Ephesians 4.11.

We must be ready for the move of God for this time and understand the level of growth and mentality we have. For this to happen, we must answer the following questions regardless of whether we are apostles, prophets, pastors, teachers, evangelists, or just believers:

- Am I ready to destroy the old mental paradigms that prevent me from understanding God's vision?

- Am I ready to make positive irreversible changes regardless of the price?

- Am I willing to take the gospel beyond my local church?

- Am I ready to abandon the "my church" mentality and adopt a Kingdom mentality?

- Am I ready to make an extreme change in my ministry in order to see the move of God?

- Am I willing to train leaders and lead them in their calling?

- Do I want to build a multi-generational church or am I satisfied reaching only this generation?

- Am I willing to change my mentality of feeding the people with the "milk" of the Word and begin to feed them the "meat" of the Word?

- Am I willing to have a flexible mind-set, a new wine mentality, to be able to participate in everything God wants to do?

- Am I willing to leave behind passivity and neutrality with the enemy and begin to fight the war against him?

- Am I ready to risk my reputation, salary, and name to see God glorified and the people blessed?

THE MINISTRY OF THE APOSTLE

These and other questions are a challenge to every believer who wants to rise to higher levels in God. Apostles will stop today's religious system from trying to shape who people are and help them renew their minds until they obtain the mind of Christ.

In conclusion, a paradigm is a negative and rigid mental structure that limits or eliminates our vision of the future. We must renew our minds and allow the Word of God and His Holy Spirit to transform our way of thinking in order to create irreversible changes in us. We must make the transition from the pastoral mentality to the apostolic mentality to receive the next great move of God. It is important for God's people and the church to make this transition; it will help us to reach, at greater levels and with greater force, the kingdom of darkness and extend the Kingdom of God to the ends of the earth.

For the next move of God to come over us, we must transform our old mentality and make irreversible changes in our lives. Pastors, evangelists, prophets, and teachers must abandon the pastoral mentality that has restricted our congregations for so long and adopt the apostolic mentality of conquest, warfare, fatherhood, and a multi-generational and multi-cultural mentality.

In these last days, we need apostles to lead the war against the army of wickedness in heavenly places and lead the edification of the body of Christ.

8

The Apostle, the Four Horns, and the Four Carpenters

One of the biggest mistakes that has affected the apostolic movement is the fact that many apostles, pastors, prophets, and evangelists became lone rangers. In other words, they separated themselves from the other Ephesians 4.11 ministries. This separation caused them to make grave mistakes in doctrine, finances, and other areas.

When a minister of God, regardless of his position, decides not to submit to anyone and to work without a spiritual covering, he will inevitably sin because he has chosen to leave and ignore the order established by God.

The Lord established the five-fold ministries listed in Ephesians 4.11 to work together, in unity, to equip the saints and destroy the powers of the enemy in each region. However, today, we rarely see that unity or relationship between the apostle and the other five-fold ministries. The reason for this is because neither the ministry of the apostle nor its function has been recognized in the body of Christ. Furthermore, the apostles that were called did not know how to relate with the prophets, teachers, pastors, or evangelists to do the job.

In the Old Testament, God mentions many truths that are relative to that time but which are also prophetic words for us. For instance, the vision prophet Zachariah received:

"¹⁸Then I raised my eyes and looked, and there were four horns. ¹⁹And I said to the angel who talked with me, "What are these?" So he answered me, "These are the horns that have scattered Judah, Israel, and Jerusalem." ²⁰Then the LORD showed me four craftsmen. ²¹And I said, "What are these coming to do?" So he said, "These are the horns that scattered Judah, so that no one could lift up his head; but the craftsmen are coming to terrify them, to cast out the horns of the nations that lifted up their horn against the land of Judah to scatter it." Zachariah 1.18-21

To have a better understanding of what happened here, let us briefly review the history of Israel:

God had spoken through the prophet Haggai to Zerubbabel, the governor of Judah, and to His people; He wanted to encourage them to build the city and the temple for Him. Around the same time, He gave the prophet Zachariah a vision which showed him that the people would begin to build again. When the prophet encouraged the people to build again, they completed the construction in four years; this was the same project that had been under construction for

14 years. Zerubbabel, the governor or Judah, had a big part in the reconstruction of the temple.

"10For who has despised the day of small things? For these seven rejoice to see the plumb line in the hand of Zerubbabel. They are the eyes of the LORD, which scan to and fro throughout the whole earth." Zachariah 4.10

This verse speaks to us in apostolic terms. When it says that Zerubbabel laid the foundation of the house, we see that this governor symbolized the apostle of the New Testament—the one who lays the foundation and builds upon it. Here, we see a truth from the Old Testament that can be applied to our time. However, in the vision given to Zachariah, there is much more we can use to help us understand the times in which we live.

"18Then I raised my eyes and looked, and there were four horns. 19And I said to the angel who talked with me, "What are these?" So he answered me, "These are the horns that have scattered Judah, Israel, and Jerusalem." Zachariah 1.18, 19

The horns in these verses represent kingdoms, the demonic powers, principalities, and the enemy's strongholds that come with two assignments:

❖ **Scatter.** These come to separate, divide, and break up Judah and the church in a thousand pieces.

❖ **Discourage.** The horns cause discouragement in the hearts of the people. Verse 21 says: *"These are the horns that scattered Judah, so that no one could lift up his head."* This is a sign of discouragement.

What is the present name for these horns or demonic powers in our nations?

1. **The spirit of intellectualism or humanism.**

   This spirit denies everything that has to do with the supernatural: miracles, healing, prophecy, and the gifts of the Holy Spirit; it reasons everything and believes in nothing that it cannot perceive through the natural senses. The philosophy of this spirit centers on man as the superior being and the mind as the source of all knowledge. This spirit operates in the minds of people, and it opens gaps for other spirits to enter and influence the way we think and live.

   ### What is the target of this horn or spirit?

   Intellectualism attacks the simple-minded or those who see everything as black or white. In the Judeo-Christian mentality, the black and white mentality is common; it is also referred to as thesis and antithesis. According to this mentality, truths and lies are parallel; they never come together. When a truth is accepted, everything else becomes a lie. For instance: Jesus is the only mediator between God and men.

"5For there is one God and one Mediator between God and men, the Man Christ Jesus, 6who gave Himself a ransom for all, to be testified in due time." 1 Timothy 2.5, 6

The Word of God is full of thesis and anti-thesis because in it, there is only one truth. However, society, which is mostly pagan, has introduced another mentality referred to as the synthetic mentality.

What is a synthetic mentality?

It is a way of thinking that argues there is something good in every sincere point of view. Therefore, it should be considered and accepted. In other words, if we truly believe in the devil, Buddha, witchcraft, or something along those lines, then what we believe, according to the synthetic mentality, must be good and therefore acceptable.

What are the consequences of this synthetic mentality?

This mentality causes people to be in a constant search for the truth but never find it. In the synthetic mentality there is no absolute truth, but rather, all truth is relative. However, the Bible only has absolute truths—black or white—there are no gray areas.

The synthetic mentality was introduced to our society by German and Greek philosophers at the end of the twentieth century; it has been influencing our society and church since then. This mentality altered the educational system of the West. Today, schools, colleges, and universities base their teachings on this type of mentality; it teaches our children and young people alternative lifestyles, that many ways lead to God, or that God is a relative truth that is easily replaceable. The synthetic mentality invaded our society at every level. Today, more than ever, it is important to fight against this horn or spirit of intellectualism and humanism and to begin to establish that the only absolute truth is God.

"5Thomas said to Him, "Lord, we do not know where You are going, and how can we know the way?" 6Jesus said to him, "I am the way, the truth, and the life. No one comes to the Father except through Me." John 14.5, 6

Today, when a person thinks in terms of black or white and declares that Jesus is the only path to heaven and eternal life, he is labeled as strange, as being narrow-minded, and a fanatic. He is told that he should consider "other" truths because these are acceptable as long as they are sincerely presented.

2. The spirit of anti-Christ.

"3...and every spirit that does not confess that Jesus Christ has come in the flesh is not of God. And this is the spirit of the Antichrist, which you have heard was coming, and is now already in the world." 1 John 4.3

God is our creator and an absolute truth. If we do not believe in an absolute truth, then we have no reason to keep living. The soul needs a firm anchor; a sense of belonging, purpose, and destiny which can only come from God. The spirit of intellectualism questions and defies the truth written in Scripture with a combination or fusion of different truths which lead men to lose their souls.

The Bible declares that every spirit that does not confess that Jesus came in the flesh is not of God—truth is more than a perception, idealism, or dream; it is a reality that cannot be changed or replaced.

What is truth?

Truth is the highest level of reality that exists in heaven, on earth, and under the earth. Jesus became flesh; tangible, touchable, solid, and visible. He can also become flesh in our bodies; He can take our sins away and save our souls. Christianity is not idealism; it is a reality—an absolute and unquestionable truth.

Truth: it is the property of being in accord with fact or reality; fidelity to an original or to a standard—without mutation; a judgment or proposition that cannot be denied rationally.

How do we confirm that what we read in Scripture is truth?

"16All Scripture is given by inspiration of God, and is profitable for doctrine, for reproof, for correction, for instruction in righteousness." 2 Timothy 3.16

When we have a synthetic mentality and question the truth in Scripture, there is no reason or value left for which to live for because outside of God's Word, there is no other absolute truth. Once we question or doubt Scripture, we lose the foundation of life; we live without limitations or moral values which lead to indecent and immoral lifestyles.

3. **The spirit of immorality.**

The third horn is the spirit of immorality which is the result of living according to the synthetic mentality. Based on this mentality, fornication, pornography, abortion, adultery, and homosexuality are viewed as normal lifestyles. When morals and principles are lost, the family is destroyed; marriage and children no longer have value or make sense—this causes anarchy in a nation.

Let us see how this spirit operates:

❖ First, the enemy opens a gap in our minds that leads us to believe that which is relative and to reject the idea of absolute truth. This way of thinking makes us tolerant and influences us to "respect" the countless truths circulating around us until they become a part of our everyday thinking.

❖ Second, this new way of thinking, tolerant and open to more truths, causes us to question the Word which is full of thesis and antithesis—black and white—truths. God's truth begins to sound extremist and intolerant so we abandon them little by little. Once this spirit infiltrates our minds, we no longer want to stand on God's Word or to be seen as strange or extremists.

❖ Finally, when this synthetic mentality takes over our minds completely, we lose our moral standards, values, and dignity. As a consequence, we begin to do things that go against nature.

"25...who exchanged the truth of God for the lie, and worshiped and served the creature rather than the Creator, who is blessed forever. Amen. 26For this reason God gave them up to vile passions. For even their women exchanged the natural use for what is against nature. 27Likewise also the men, leaving the natural use of the woman, burned in their lust for one another, men with men committing what is shameful, and receiving in themselves the penalty of their error which was due."
Romans 1.25-27

❖ This spirit or third horn leads to total destruction; its goal is to lead us away from God and to have us focus on natural things.

4.   The spirit of lust or materialism.

"9But those who desire to be rich fall into temptation and a snare, and into many foolish and harmful lusts which drown men in destruction and perdition. 10For the love of money is a root of all kinds of evil, for which some have strayed from the faith in their greediness, and pierced themselves through with many sorrows." 1 Timothy 6.9, 10

This spirit attacks by pushing people to seek wealth; it creates in them the compulsive insatiable desire to have more. Lust leads to wanting more and more material things to satisfy a desire of the flesh. However, the more people accumulate, the less satisfied they feel, and the emptiness in them seems larger and deeper each day.

This spirit has destroyed many ministries; it is the uncontrolled desire for wealth that causes us to forget God and spiritual things. The goal of this spirit is to take us out of balance and cause us to lust wealth. This does not mean we cannot be rich; of course we can. God wants to bless us with material wealth so we can contribute to the advancement of His Kingdom and have in abundance to help others.

These are the four horns that Zachariah saw, the demons that scattered Judah, and they are the same that are trying to destroy our society and moral values. We need to take a stand and destroy the demons of pornography, the love of money, and intellectualism which are dividing our families. The horn of humanism attacks those who choose to adopt the black and white mentality; the horn of anti-Christ questions His Word; the spirit of immorality attacks our moral values and the family; the horn of lust turns our hearts towards wealth. We should remember that God is the absolute truth; that His Word is eternal, that it will never pass away, that our values are founded on Scripture, and that our wealth is found in seeking the Kingdom of God.

God Raises the Four Carpenters

Today, many of God's people are discouraged and divided due to the influence of the four horns or demonic powers mentioned earlier. We need the power to defeat them and destroy them once and for all from our society. That is why God revealed the four carpenters to Zachariah in the same vision. They represent the ministries found in Ephesians 4.11: the prophet, teacher, pastor, and evangelist. These are called and trained to defeat and rebuke the four spirits and to help build the people of God. And yet, why are there four and not five? Where is the apostle?

We know the apostle is the master builder with the qualities of an administrator. In other words, we have four men with skills to build, and the fifth, the apostle, with these same skills plus the leadership ability to bring together and lead the four carpenters and show them how to work the right way. These five offices constitute the hand of God; together, they will build for God and destroy the four horns as seen in the diagram in chapter 6.

Illustration: to raise a building, we need four types of skilled individuals: a carpenter, electrician, plumber, and bricklayer. Imagine for just a moment that one of the four has the gift of administration, leadership, and who is preparing to become on architect. This man has knowledge in all the four areas mentioned plus the ability to coordinate the work of the others—that is an apostle.

The apostle comes from the four offices; he has the ability to see God's complete plan and knows what He wants to build and how He wants it done. Furthermore, he has the ability of leadership which draws near other leaders to join the team while he supervises the construction of the house of God.

Why does God send these four carpenters?

God raises four carpenters to carry out two things:

❖ To terrorize and make the four horns tremble.
❖ To destroy and cast them out.

One reason why the enemy has opposed the restoration of the five-fold ministries is because he knows that when these are completely restored, the horns he has assigned to the cities and to the nations will be destroyed and the Kingdom of God will take dominion; hence, the importance of the restoration of the apostolic ministry. The four carpenters must rebuke the four horns with the leading of the apostolic spirit.

We must build apostolic churches with the ability to raise prophets, pastors, evangelists, and teachers capable of destroying the horns that want to divide God's people. Now we understand why we have not been able to destroy the spirits of humanism, anti-Christ, immorality, and lust; because we have not used God's hand which is the only one capable and powerful enough to destroy these horns and build the Kingdom of God on earth.

Without the leadership of an apostle, it will be very difficult to destroy the four horns.

If we continue reading the book of Zachariah, the second chapter teaches that the main reason for the existence of these carpenters is to build a spiritual city after the horns are destroyed.

"¹Then I raised my eyes and looked, and behold, a man with a measuring line in his hand. ²So I said, "where are you going?" And he said to me, "To measure Jerusalem, to see what is its width and what is its length." ³And there was the angel who talked with me, going out; and another angel was coming out to meet him, ⁴who said to him, "Run, speak to this young man, saying: 'Jerusalem shall be inhabited as towns without walls, because of the multitude of men and livestock in it. ⁵For I,' says the LORD, 'will be a wall of fire all around her, and I will be the glory in her midst.'""
Zachariah 2.1-5

The carpenters are going to build a spiritual city with the exact measurements given by God.

In other words, an apostle overseeing the four ministries to build according to the divine plan. This is apostolic! The city that Zachariah saw was made up of many little towns; it had no walls because of the multitude, and it was surrounded by a wall of fire. It did not have a rock wall but was encircled by the glory of God. The prophet saw a city built by God, and the glory surrounding it was equivalent to the one around David's Tabernacle. This is the place where the five-fold ministries of Ephesians 4.11 should seek the face of God.

God's plan, since the Old Testament, was to raise apostles capable of building spiritual cities; individuals who would receive the plan for the city, the New Jerusalem from heaven, and establish it on earth. Abraham saw the city that was built upon the foundation that was created by God.

"8By faith Abraham obeyed when he was called to go out to the place which he would receive as an inheritance. And he went out, not knowing where he was going. 9By faith he dwelt in the land of promise as in a foreign country, dwelling in tents with Isaac and Jacob, the heirs with him of the same promise; 10for he waited for the city which has foundations, whose builder and maker is God." Hebrews 11.8-10

❖ That city was the carbon copy of the heavenly Jerusalem.

"²²But you have come to Mount Zion and to the city of the living God, the heavenly Jerusalem, to an innumerable company of angels." Hebrews 12.22

❖ Jesus saw the city.

"¹³You are the salt of the earth; but if the salt loses its flavor, how shall it be seasoned? It is then good for nothing but to be thrown out and trampled underfoot by men. ¹⁴You are the light of the world. A city that is set on a hill cannot be hidden. ¹⁵Nor do they light a lamp and put it under a basket, but on a lampstand, and it gives light to all who are in the house." Matthew 5.13-15

That city is the design of the heavenly Jerusalem which is build by the four carpenters and directed by an apostle. The apostle raises an apostolic church according to the heavenly design which, according to what Jesus said, has to do with three things:

Salt. In the natural, salt is the main ingredient used to give food flavor and to keep it from spoiling. The salt of the Kingdom, which is capable of penetrating society, is the Christian full of God's power; he seasons it with the joy, light, and righteousness of the Kingdom—the

Christian that is the salt of the earth stops corruption from taking over society.

Light. The light is the life of the Kingdom that shines through a Christian. This light is the good testimony of his actions, the transparency of his life, the integrity with which he conducts his affairs, and the righteousness of the believer which shines on the life of those who are in darkness; this light draws others to God.

City. The power of God is concentrated in a place where His government is established. He gives the church of the city a special authority to transform society; hence, the reason why God wants to raise churches in the city.

What are the characteristics of a city church?

- It is visible and cannot hide.

- It is strong and powerful.

- It has greater resources for prayer, evangelism, the gifts, deliverance, discipleship, the ministries, and finances.

- It provides adequate training in the development of apostles, prophets, evangelists, teachers, and pastors.

- It exerts its influence and authority over society.

- It is able to create strategies and offer its resources to help the region, nation, and even other nations.

- It is capable of exercising its spiritual authority over an area and cleanses the heavenly realm of all the wicked strongholds that govern in that place.

The five-fold ministry of Ephesians 4.11 make the body function in the area of their particular gift, and that is why they have the ability to build the city.

❖ Prophets not only prophesy but can also detect the gifts in others; their goal is to help them develop those gifts and teach them how to use them to produce a church that will bring the voice of God to the city.

❖ Evangelists not only evangelize but also detect the gift of the evangelist in others; they help to develop that gift, teach them to use it, and the result is a people or church trained and equipped to reach the lost.

❖ Pastors are able to take care of a church with thousands of believers, without stress, because they can identify, develop, train, and teach the believers how to work by using the pastoral gift. The result is a leadership team with the ability to take care of the people.

❖ Teachers not only teach but also identify the gift of teaching in others; they develop that gift and teach the people how to use it to produce a church that teaches God's Word.

In a city church, the five-fold ministries of Ephesians 4.11 focus mainly on the vision, strategies, principles, concepts, and doctrine, not on the small details or on the everyday situations that might arise in the church.

There are large churches in a city that no one knows exist because they are neither salt nor light for the city. Therefore, a city church is not defined only by its size, though they are most likely larger than a local church or even a mega church, but by its effectiveness and contribution to the city through the five-fold ministries.

God is currently raising the five-fold ministries of Ephesians 4.11—the four carpenters which are led by the apostle—so they can build powerful apostolic churches capable of terrorizing, destroying, and eliminating the four horns. In the same way that Abraham saw one land, one people, and one city, which would be the bridge needed to take possession of the inheritance and gather the harvest, we must also believe in the vision that God gives us and work hard to possess our land and inheritance. If we do not build a spiritual city—apostolic churches—we will never take possession of the whole harvest. As an apostle, my passion is to identify, affirm, teach, and train prophets, pastors, evangelists, and teachers and bring them together as a powerful force to destroy and eliminate the strongholds that try to stop or slow down the move of God. I want to join forces with them, so that together, we can build strong and powerful apostolic centers of the city and with them gather the end-time harvest. Praise God!

Bibliography

Alan Vincent, Outpouring Ministries. 8308
    Fredericksburg Road, San Antonio, TX 78229.

Biblia de Estudio Arco Iris. Reina Valera 1960;
    Nashville, Tennessee: Broadman & Holman
    Publishers, 1995.

Biblia Plenitud. Reina Valera 1960; Nashville,
    Tennessee: Caribe Editorial, 1994.

Blue Letter Bible. April 12, 2006.
    http://www.blueletterbible.org/index.html

Diccionario Español a Inglés, Inglés a Español. Num.
    81; Dinamarca, Mexico: Larousse Editorial,
    1993.

El Pequeño Larousse Ilustrado, Larousse ed.
    Barcelona: Editorial Spes, 2002.

James Strong, *The New Strong's Exhaustive
    Concordance of the Bible*. Nashville, Tennessee:
    Thomas Nelson, 2001.

Lock A. Ward, *Nuevo Diccionario de la Biblia*.
    Miami, Florida: Unilit Editorial, 1999.

Biblia Reina Valera 1995. Edición de Estudio; USA.:
   Sociedades Biblicas Unidas, 1998.

The Amplified Bible. Grand Rapids, Michigan:
   Zondervan, 1987.

The New American Standard Version. n.p.:
   Zondervan, n.d.

*The Tormont Webster's Illustrated Encyclopedic
   Dictionary.* n.p.: Tormont Publications, 1990.

W.E. Vine, *Diccionario Expositivo de las Palabras del
   Antiguo Testamento y Nuevo Testamento.*
   Nashville, Tennessee: Thomas Nelson, 1999.
   ISBN: 0-89922-495-4.

*Webster's New World International Spanish
   Dictionary English/Spanish.* Indianapolis,
   Indiana: Wiley Publishing, Inc, 2004.

ERJ PUBLICATIONS

SUPERNATURAL EVANGELISM
Guillermo Maldonado

This book will challenge you to win souls for Christ and teach you how to present God's powerful message of salvation by using the method established by the most influential evangelist of all ages: Jesus!

ISBN: 1-59272-088-9 | 134 pp.

BIBLICAL FOUNDATIONS FOR NEW BELIEVERS
Guillermo Maldonado

This book will guide your first steps as you experience your new life as a born-again believer; it will help you to grow and understand every step of your new journey in Christ.

ISBN: 1-59272-089-7 | 96 pp.

THE FAMILY
Guillermo Maldonado

Your responsibilities in the home, how to communicate, being single and satisfied, how to raise wonderful children, and much more is what you can expect to find in this eye-opening book which will answer every question you ever had about marriage and the family.

ISBN: 1-59272-089-0 | 162 pp.

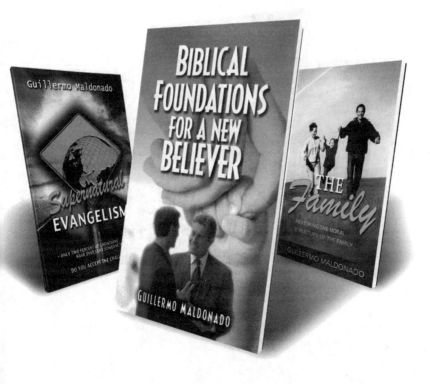

ERJ PUBLICATIONS

OVERCOMING DEPRESSION

Guillermo Maldonado

This book, written in line with God's Word, will help you understand the root of depression and how to overcome it; it will show you how to make the best of every situation in your life and give you the victory!

ISBN: 1-59272-141-2
68 pp.

DISCOVER YOUR PURPOSE AND CALLING IN GOD

Guillermo Maldonado

Are you ready to take the challenge and discover God's purpose for your life? And when you discover that truth, then what? This book describes, in detail, the five-fold ministries and the gifts of the Holy Spirit. Find your place in God's army, today!

ISBN: 1-59272-094-3

FORGIVENESS

Guillermo Maldonado

It is impossible to avoid being offended. At some point in your life, you must choose to forgive those who hurt you. If your desire is to live a powerful, victorious, spirit-filled life, this book will help you do just that!

ISBN: 1-59272-040-4 | 76 pp.

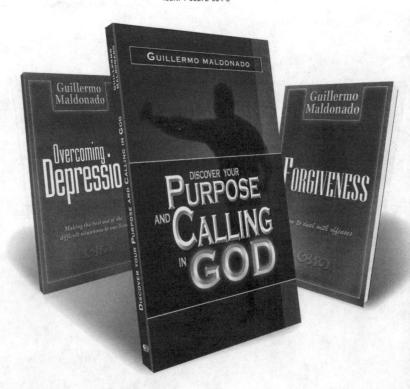

ERJ PUBLICATIONS

LEADERS THAT CONQUER

Guillermo Maldonado

Learn how to confront effectively, how to delegate authority, and the price of being a good leader. This book will help you to overcome every limitation set before you and challenge you to be a leader that conquers!

ISBN: 1-59272-023-4 | 206 pp.

INNER HEALING AND DELIVERANCE

Guillermo Maldonado

Unforgiveness, bitterness, rejection, guilt, schizophrenia, how demons gain entry into our lives, and more are only a few of the many subjects you will find in this book. This "how-to" manual will help you to understand those areas of your life that need to be confronted and give you the certainty that only the Lord and His revealed truth can set you completely free.

ISBN: 1-59272-007-2 | 269 pp.

THE HOLY ANOINTING

Guillermo Maldonado

This book provides basic principles for ministering and flowing in the anointing, which is the manifestation of the Holy Spirit. If we learn to flow in it, we will minister effectively and see supernatural results.

ISBN: 1-59272-038-2
158 pp.

ERJ PUBLICATIONS

HOW TO RETURN TO OUR FIRST LOVE

Guillermo Maldonado

Sometimes, we fail to recognize that the cares and anxieties of this world affect our relationship with God; we get so involved in serving God that we forget to nurture our relationship with our Heavenly Father. This book will help you light the fire of your love for God, once more, and keep it going strong in order to have victory over all things.

ISBN: 1-59272-162-1

PRAYER

Guillermo Maldonado

Renew your interest and learn how to go into deeper levels of prayer as you develop a close and intimate relationship with God; this book will help you to succeed in your ministry and in all facets of life.

ISBN: 1-59272-090-0
180 pp.

THE CHARACTER OF A LEADER

Guillermo Maldonado

God wants to shape your character! Many men and women of God are destroyed because of lack of integrity; they are not transparent in thought, behavior, or lifestyle. They failed because they neglected to change and improve their character and charisma. Allow God, through this book, to shape your character and become all you can be!

ISBN: 1-59272-061-3

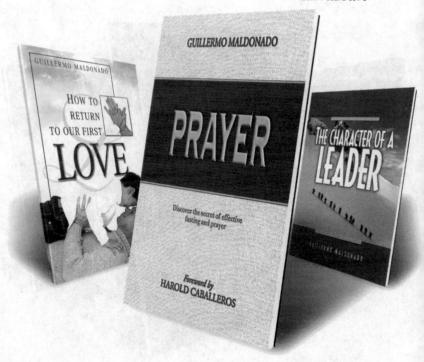

ERJ PUBLICATIONS

SPIRITUAL MATURITY

Guillermo Maldonado

Learn to be all that God wants you to be by identifying the different levels of spiritual maturity and by discovering which level you are in.

ISBN 1-59272-192-7

THE NEW WINE GENERATION

Guillermo Maldonado

The New Wine generation, under the anointing and the power of the Holy Spirit, must conquer and take back what the enemy has stolen from us. This book will instruct and inspire you to walk in the spiritual realm and to destroy all works of evil.

ISBN: 1-59272-039-0
195 pp.

HOW TO HEAR THE VOICE OF GOD

Guillermo Maldonado

Do you know God's voice? After you read this book, you will be able to discern God's voice and learn to walk in the supernatural will of God.

ISBN: 1-59272-091-9
156 pp.